TRUSTING LIFE

TRUSTING LIFE

Overcoming the Fear and Beliefs
That Block Peace and Happiness

GINA LAKE

Endless Satsang Foundation

Endless Satsang Foundation

www.radicalhappiness.com

Cover photograph: © Andrejas Pidjass/Dreamstime.com

ISBN: 978-1463596194

Copyright © 2011 by Gina Lake

CONTENTS

INTRODUCTION

In my work with individuals over the years, I've come to realize just how important trusting life is. It is often a lack of such trust that blocks true happiness and peace and makes it difficult to live the life we were meant to live. We don't naturally trust life. There's a reason for this, and those who've experienced any amount of abuse or wounding in childhood find it especially hard. This distrust makes it difficult to be in the moment, where peace and happiness abide. How can anyone drop their guard and enjoy life when they're afraid of life?

Fear and distrust are the enemies of life. Fear pretends to protect us, but it limits and immobilizes us and takes the joy out of life. Fear and distrust don't keep us safe. Rather, they keep us lost in our thoughts, in our internal reality, and out of the present moment—reality. For this reason, fear and distrust are actually dysfunctional, not functional, as they may seem to be.

Fear and distrust are the greatest hurdles to seeing the truth about life—that it is good, abundant, supportive, and potentially joyous. The truth about life is really good news. The truth could be the opposite, and sometimes life does feel that way. But fortunately, goodness is at the core of life, and that is what this book will offer evidence for.

Overcoming the fear and beliefs that keep you from discovering and experiencing this goodness is some of the most important emotional and spiritual work you'll ever do. There's nothing more important than seeing the truth about life. As they say, "The truth will set you free," and what it sets you free from is the fear and distrust that belong to the ego. It actually sets you free from the ego itself.

Another name for the ego is the false self because it isn't who we really are, but only *ideas* about who we are: "I'm a woman," "I'm a shopkeeper," "I like horses," "I'm artistic," "I was abused," "I'm going to be famous," "I have to have nice things," "No one understands me," "I'm different," "I'm a good cook," "I can't do anything right," "I don't like to travel," "I'm lazy."

The ego is the aspect of ourselves that provides us with a sense of being an individual, and for that it is useful. However, the ego, through our thoughts, attempts to manage our life, but it is a poor manager, a poor guide to life. We are here to discover the truth about life, the truth about who we really are, and how to live from a deeper place than the ego, from a place that is often called the Heart, which I also call *Essence*—our true self. This discovery is what this book is about.

One of the most difficult things about moving from living from the ego to living from Essence is overcoming the ego's distrust and trusting that there's something else besides the ego to trust—Essence. One would think that trusting Essence would be natural, even easy, since Essence is our natural state.

But it seems that we're programmed to trust something else. We're programmed to trust the ego, to trust the thoughts that go through our mind—the voice in our head.

The commentary we hear in our head that appears to be our thoughts is what many call the *egoic mind.* It's called that because it is the aspect of the mind that belongs to the ego. It's different from the aspect of the mind we use to read a book, add a column of numbers, design something, solve a problem, follow directions, and do all of the other mental tasks that help us function. I call this the *functional mind.* We need this more functional aspect of the mind, which is like a tool we pick up and use and put down when we're done using it. But we actually don't need the egoic mind, which appears to be our own voice, and yet it actually belongs to nobody. When we look, we find nobody behind it.

The egoic mind merely reflects our conditioning and the conclusions we've come to based on our own and other people's experiences, and other beliefs, opinions, and personal perceptions as well as fears, desires, and judgments. This voice isn't the origin of any wisdom we've gained nor of our insights and intuitions. Such things don't originate in the mind, but are experienced or sensed more subtly in the body, often in the Heart or gut.

Wisdom, insights, and intuitions appear as a knowing, an "Aha!" or a sense of rightness about something—we just know something or suddenly have clarity about something. Some might call such knowings faith, but these knowings aren't based on an idea or a belief we've been taught, as religious faith often is, but on a deeper knowing within us that comes from connection with Essence. Unlike beliefs, such knowings show up in the moment when they're needed.

There's something within us that guides us, but it doesn't do so through the voice in our head, but through deeper, more subtle nudges, inspiration, intuitions, urges, and exuberance of spirit. So while the voice in our head attempts to guide us, there's something else—Essence—that's guiding us more wisely and truly that's far more trustworthy than the voice in our head.

It's funny that we think of the voice in our head as our own and that we tend to believe it and value what it says, when so often it's contradictory, unhelpful, and unkind. We are so much wiser than this voice! We are so much kinder and more courageous than this voice, which is often fearful and upset with life. My hope is that this book will help you not be ruled by the petty, fearful voice of the ego and that you will more deeply come to trust your own beautiful true self, which has always been the only thing living your life, while the false self has seemed to be who you are. We are all much wiser, more loving, and greater than we seem to be, and it's possible to discover this now.

I invite you to explore the greatest mystery of all—who you really are. But this will only be possible if you're willing to trust something other than the thoughts that run through your mind. I will give you many good reasons to not trust these thoughts and to trust, instead, the beautiful Being that you are, which is alive in you. That is my purpose in writing this, and your success rests only on your willingness to entertain the possibility that you are much more than what you *think* about yourself.

Gina Lake
July, 2011
Sedona, Arizona

CHAPTER 1
The Importance of Trusting Life

BELIEFS ARE SELF-FULFILLING PROPHECIES

No one would argue the benefits of a stable, loving, nurturing home life to a child's development and future success. We all know how important these things are to human beings. The reason they are important is that they provide the child with a sense that he or she can trust others and trust life. Without such an environment, people grow up believing that others and life won't support them or be kind to them, that others and life don't care about them.

Children who grow up believing that they can do anything, that they are lovable and capable, and that life is an exciting adventure to be explored and enjoyed experience life very differently from those who grow up believing the opposite. Children who are loved and properly cared for are gifted with the sense that whatever happens, things will turn out alright. Those who don't have this experience in childhood often lack this sense of safety and security or expect the worst. Distrust robs them of their sense of possibility and "Yes, I can!" This is a great disadvantage.

Beliefs are very often self-fulfilling prophecies: They color what we're experiencing, and this affects how we respond to others and to life, which in turn affects what happens next. Often whatever happens next creates a feedback loop that reinforces our beliefs. A simple example is if you believe that people are rude and someone accidently bumps into you on a crowded street, you're likely to interpret that as rudeness and react angrily toward them. Your reaction is likely to elicit an unfriendly, if not angry, response from them, which reinforces your belief that people are rude. You actually created an unpleasant situation without realizing it by your incorrect assumption.

Here's a more general example. People who believe that life is good and trustworthy act as if this is so, and they don't let fear or life's difficulties stop them. They don't take difficulties personally and feel persecuted by them or define difficulties as insurmountable problems. Difficulties are accepted as a normal part of life, as challenges that can be learned from along the road to success. The success that results from this attitude reinforces their belief in the goodness of life.

On the other hand, those who are distrustful of life and of themselves, let their fear and distrust stop them before they even get started. Any difficulties are experienced as proof of their unworthiness and the harshness of life. Instead of moving past difficulties, they allow themselves to be defeated by them, thereby reinforcing their belief that life can't be trusted and they won't ever be happy or have what they want.

Our beliefs create a mental and emotional state that is peaceful or unpeaceful, content or discontent, accepting or angry, happy or unhappy, loving or unloving, fearless or fearful. Our beliefs are very powerful—if we believe them. They create an internal reality, or internal emotional climate. They also influence external reality—what we do, how we behave, how others respond to us, what opportunities come to us, and what opportunities we take advantage of. Those who grow up with beliefs that cause them to fear and distrust life live with an internal state that not only is uncomfortable, but also blocks them from experiencing love, abundance, happiness, and peace.

No one deserves a less happy and less fulfilling life than is possible, but that's what many experience who are caught in fear and distrust. And, of course, the results of their fear and distrust reinforce their negative beliefs about themselves and life. That's the unfortunate situation many find themselves in.

It doesn't have to be that way. It's possible to overcome the fear and distrust that interfere with a happy and an abundant life. It's really good news that we have some control over our internal state. There are many things about life we can't control, but we do have some control over—and responsibility for—our internal state. We can learn to modify it and so change our inner and outer realities.

Here's another example of how distrust can become a self-fulfilling prophecy and be reinforced. Many children grow up unloved and so conclude that they are unlovable. If you couldn't trust your parents to love and support you, then why would you trust others to love you or life to support you? You'd feel like you're on your own in life, even while you see others being loved and taken care of. You're likely to feel separate and apart from others, like they have something you don't have and will never have—they can be happy, but not you.

If you feel this way, then when others approach you, you may doubt their interest in you. You may even feel like they'll hurt you, although you may be unconscious of assuming this. As a result, you're likely to be shy, cautious, and closed instead of friendly, warm, open, and giving. So how do others respond to that? Most likely, they won't pursue getting to know you. Even someone who's generally open and friendly might not be that way toward someone who appears uninviting and unapproachable.

When we are withholding, withdrawn, and cautious, others tend to be withholding, withdrawn, and cautious toward us. Then the beliefs that we aren't lovable, don't belong, and won't be supported are reinforced, and feeling lovable and open to others becomes even more difficult. Being distrusting and fearful tends to bring out the same in others.

Fortunately, this goes for more positive states as well: When we're warm, friendly, kind, and caring, that also tends to be how others respond to us. What we put out, we tend to get back. Distrust and fear don't bring us the life we want or deserve, while the opposite—trust and love—do. Distrust and fear are anti-life, while trust and love are the essence of life.

Many people are caught in this bind: Distrusting others and distrusting life create experiences that reinforce that distrust. Here's another example: Because they don't trust that life will support them through work they love, many take whatever job comes along, a job they are ill-suited for, or a job just because it pays well. Although there may be times when we need to take such jobs temporarily, for many, these types of jobs become a permanent career. When we are in work that we aren't suited for or don't like, we're bound to be unhappy, not perform at our best, and not feel good about ourselves. These feelings reinforce the original sense of life not being good, supportive, abundant, or potentially happy.

Contrast this experience with someone who doesn't settle for just any job but pursues work that excites and interests him or her. Every step of this process requires trust: The person has to trust the drive to do that kind of work, trust that he or she can follow through on the many hours of study and training required, and trust that there will be a job available. No one can know for sure how this will turn out, but the desire to do that work doesn't stand a chance of being fulfilled without trust every step of the way.

Those who distrust themselves and life are likely to distrust their longing to do a particular kind of work. Even if they do trust that longing, they might sabotage the fulfillment of this dream by distrusting their ability to complete the training, to find a job, or to do well at it. People who distrust life find reasons to not pursue what they really want to do. Then what they're left with is something they don't want to do, something that can't make them happy.

TRUSTING YOUR HEART

Everyone deserves to be happy. In part, this happiness depends on living the life you were meant to live. What I mean by this is that everyone has a unique part to play in the Whole. When we're playing that part, we feel fulfilled and happy; when we aren't, we feel depressed and lost. Playing this part requires that we follow our Heart, or what I call *Essence*, because it's through the Heart that our part in the Whole is communicated to us.

Following our Heart is the key to happiness, and distrusting the longings and impulses of the Heart is the greatest block to happiness. Following our Heart isn't something we learn to do in school, but it's more important than anything school has to teach because if you don't follow your Heart, you'll be out of step with the Whole, and whatever else you do won't fulfill you.

The trouble is our Heart doesn't speak to us as directly and clearly as our thoughts, which are often at odds with our Heart. So too often we listen to our thoughts instead of our Heart. Our thoughts—the ongoing commentary in our head—come from a very different place than the Heart. The thoughts that run through our mind are primarily our ego's thoughts and represent the conditioning, programming, or imprinting we took on or were given.

Because this aspect of the mind—the voice in our head—belongs to the ego, it is often called the *egoic mind*. It is the aspect of the mind that is used by the ego. Although we think of these thoughts as our own thoughts, they actually belong to the conditioned, or false, self—the ego—and not to our true self, or Essence, which doesn't generally communicate to us through thought but through other means, particularly intuition. Unfortunately, the ego doesn't have the answers to how to live life. Conditioning is just information and beliefs, which can't provide wise guidance about how to live our life. And yet, we often allow such thoughts to determine our direction and actions.

If we were completely cut off from our Heart, or Essence, then such thoughts would be all we had to guide us. Fortunately, no one is ever entirely cut off from their Heart, although it can seem that way. The Heart is always available and communicates through inspiration, insights, intuitions, drives, inner nudges, and other ways. It communicates in many different ways, and we are often influenced by it, whether we're aware of that influence or not. In any moment, our thoughts may be trying to move us in a particular direction, while our Heart is either going along with that or sending its own message about some other direction.

The Heart is the wise master. Its job is to direct us to fulfill our part in the Whole. Following its messages will feel good, right, and fulfilling because those feelings are the reward for playing the part we're meant to play in the Whole. The ego has another agenda, however. It seeks safety, security, pleasure, comfort, power, and control. There's a place for these things, of course, but getting them doesn't equal happiness or fulfillment.

True happiness is experienced when we're aligned with Essence and following our Heart, and quite the opposite is true when we're identified with the egoic mind: We feel discontent, with a sense of never having enough or being enough. When we are identified with the ego, we experience the ego's distrust, fear, dissatisfaction, and drives for security, safety, pleasure, comfort, power, status, recognition, money, possessions, and control. The ego and Essence represent two very different states of consciousness, or ways of being. One is a state of dissatisfaction and the other is a state of peace and contentment.

Identification with the ego is the state most people are in most of the time, while Essence tends to be a brief and passing experience. Moments of being in Essence are the most beautiful moments we experience as humans. They are marked by feelings of love, unity with all life, contentment, peace, and gratitude. These are the moments we all want more of, but this state, although it is our natural state, is illusive for most people, only because the egoic mind is so compelling, so convincing, and so pervasive.

But it doesn't have to be this way. We are meant to discover or, rather, rediscover our true nature and express that in the world. We are meant to see through the false self and express our true self. This requires both seeing the truth about the thoughts that run through our mind and realizing the presence of something else that is beyond thought—our true nature. This realization isn't possible without first letting go of some degree of attachment, identification with, and belief in the voice in our head, the egoic mind. What's required is a new relationship to this voice, one that is more objective.

It is very difficult to establish such a new and radical relationship with our egoic mind without trust in the goodness of life and in the presence of something more real and true than the false self. However, the ego keeps us identified with it with fearful, doubting, distrusting thoughts. The ego doesn't trust life, and it convinces us that life is untrustworthy and that to stay safe, we must listen to *it*—we must trust the ego.

We will never come to trust life if we are trusting the thoughts that run through our mind because these thoughts don't trust life. Before we can learn to trust something else, we first have to see that the egoic mind isn't worthy of our trust. But fear is very convincing! The egoic mind keeps us believing it by scaring us. It tells us we won't be safe if we don't listen to it and do as it suggests: "You'll end up on the street if you don't take that job!" The ego assumes there's nothing else guiding life—but there is! How can we discover this Mystery at the core of life if we continue to believe the egoic mind, which doesn't believe in this Mystery?

PLAYING YOUR PART IN THE WHOLE

There's something else here to trust besides the untrustworthy egoic mind. There's something loving, good, and trustworthy behind all of life that's beyond our wildest imagination, and we are not only part of it, we *are* it! The Whole that I'm speaking about is the sum total of all creation, including that which created it all.

The Creator doesn't stand apart from creation but is alive within creation, in everything. Everything that exists is part of the Creator—the Oneness—and that Creator is reveling in its creations. It designed creation—the Whole—to support its creations. It also designed creation to be its playground and learning ground. This view of the Creator and creation can help you trust life and be more happy, loving, and at peace. Does your current view of the Creator and creation do that?

Each of us is perfectly designed for what we came here to do. We have unique talents and traits that the Whole means to use. The Whole wouldn't be the same without each of us! We are each other's teachers and helpers. You could think of the Whole, the Oneness, as a body and each of us as its cells, which perform specific functions. Each cell needs to perform the function it was designed to do, not some other function. Likewise, each of us has a purpose within the Whole. Serving that purpose helps the Whole function as it's meant to, and happiness comes from doing that. Some people function as presidents and leaders, while others grow and cook the food, transport goods, heal the sick, invent and discover things, build and design things, raise and teach the children, clean and maintain things, make and enforce the laws, and inspire and uplift. Some serve as change-makers and revolutionaries, while others preserve the status quo and tradition. The list of functions and roles is endless.

Even those who don't seem to be contributing in practical ways contribute in spiritual ways: Those who are disabled, dependent, or mentally ill provide growthful challenges and opportunities for us to serve and to develop our compassion, patience, courage, and other qualities. There isn't a single person on the planet who isn't here for a reason and who isn't performing some function for the Whole. Even those who aren't fulfilling the function they were meant to still have an impact on the Whole and therefore evolve it.

How is it that someone can be out of touch with what he or she is here to do and learn? The answer is: the ego. The ego can keep us from being fully in touch with the Whole and with Essence, which guides us in fulfilling our life purpose. As a result, the ego provides a marvelous challenge for humanity, and the ego was designed to do exactly that.

We were given an egoic mind because it serves a purpose within the Whole. The ego, through the egoic mind, creates the suffering that fuels much of our activity, emotional growth, and spiritual evolution. Suffering is built into our world (perhaps not all worlds!) by the Oneness and serves a purpose in creation. Suffering is also ultimately what wakes us up out of the egoic state of consciousness and points us back to our true self, to the Oneness behind all life. We are meant to have an ego, *and* it is our greatest challenge.

THE ROLE OF SUFFERING

In this world there is polarity, or duality: light and dark, love and fear, happiness and sadness. Darkness helps us know and appreciate the light: Hatred, fear, sadness, and suffering help us know and appreciate love, peace, joy, and the absence of suffering. This polarity serves the Oneness. It provides an arena for experiences, growth, and learning. More importantly, it provides a means by which human beings can rediscover their original nature.

Within creation, the Oneness is exploring and playing, learning and evolving. It created what it has created for its own joy, adventure, and evolution. To participate fully in its creation, the Oneness had to lose itself in creation and forget itself as Oneness. It created a multitude of beings that it could lose itself in that were conscious so that it could be aware of and interact with what it created. To have a fully fresh experience, the Oneness had to lose awareness of itself as All That Is and believe it is a separate being. But it was also careful not to permanently lose itself in creation. It designed a way to eventually return to its original state of Oneness. Suffering is the means by which the Oneness rediscovers itself. Suffering points the way Home. Let me explain...

The ego is the sense we have of being a separate person. That's what the ego was designed for, in part, and what it gives us—a sense of being *me*. This sense of being an individual is accomplished through all the thoughts we have about ourselves: "I like this and not that," "I want this and not that," "I'm this way and not that way," "I need this and not that."

Who is this "I"? Where do all those thoughts come from? When you look deeply into these questions, you see that this "I" is like a mirage—there isn't anything or anyone behind or beyond the thought "I," although it seems like there is. There's no entity that the thought "I" belongs to. "I" is just a thought. This is the illusion created by the Oneness so that it could have the experiences it is having within creation. We really aren't separate individuals, although it seems like we are, and herein lies the suffering—in part.

The trouble with being a *me* is that it's a lie—it's not the truth about who we really are. Who we really are isn't actually a separate person (we are the Oneness); we are only playing at being separate. This sense of separation, because it is a lie, causes suffering. It doesn't feel good to be separate and apart from our true nature, although experiencing itself this way for the time being serves the Oneness.

This sense of separation is at the heart of the ego's discontentment and unhappiness and all of its seeking. When we are identified with the ego (i.e., when we are believing that the voice in our head is our own, true voice), we are discontent and unhappy because we are disconnected from our true nature, from love and peace. At a certain point in our evolution, we realize the pain of this and become disillusioned with the power, money, and other things the ego goes after to try to be happy, while never really finding true happiness. That's when we begin seeking the truth about who we really are.

When we are identified with the ego, we suffer not only because we are disconnected from our true nature, but also because the ego's solutions for this suffering don't work. The ego leads us to believe that if only we had more of something—more love, beauty, recognition, status, money, power, success, security, safety, possessions, youth, health—we could finally rest and be happy and at peace. But many of us have realized that there's no end to what the ego wants and thinks it needs to be happy: As soon as we get something the "I" wants, the "I" wants more of it or something else.

The ego is this ongoing sense of dissatisfaction and sense of not having or being enough, and the ego's unhappiness will never be assuaged by anything in the material world or by anything we can achieve or become. Peace can only be attained by dropping out of the egoic mind and into Essence, where we can once again experience our connection with all of life, with the Oneness that we are. Only this connection with our true self really satisfies.

Another reason we suffer when we're identified with the egoic mind is we believe the egoic mind's lies and half-truths, which often make us feel bad. So many of our thoughts stir up negative feelings! Most of our unpleasant emotions are caused by our thoughts, although we aren't always conscious of these thoughts: "I'll never succeed," "I can't do it," "I'll never be loved," "I'm not smart enough," "He never treats me right," "She doesn't care about me." Although there may be a grain of truth in such thoughts, they're limited and limiting stories we tell ourselves that lead to all sorts of unpleasant and unnecessary emotions. Our egoic mind is apparently in the business of causing us suffering!

To summarize, the ego is at the root of suffering because:

- The ego provides the sense of separation from the Oneness that we are and that we long to return to.

- The ego is never satisfied and points us in directions that don't lead to happiness or an end to dissatisfaction, only to more dissatisfaction.

- The ego is a voice of negativity that generates unpleasant emotions and often drives unwise, unnecessary, self-destructive, or harmful actions.

The good news is that, although we have an ego, we don't have to identify with it—we don't have to listen to the voice in our head. We can see it for what it is, dismiss it, and turn our attention elsewhere. When we do stop listening to this voice, we drop into the moment, and Essence is experienced. The suffering of ego identification motivates us to find a way out of this suffering, and the way out is disidentifying with the egoic mind. Disidentifying with the egoic mind automatically drops us into Essence and brings us the experience of our true nature. Instead of experiencing our usual limited sense of self, we experience the sense of freedom, expansion, peace, love, and absence of self-concern that marks our true nature.

Suffering points the way Home by pointing us away from the ego. Suffering is the "stick," and the joy and peace of Essence are the "carrot" that move us from the ego to Essence. Suffering is the Oneness's plan for returning us to our true nature. If we were to continue to trust the ego instead of life, we'd never make it Home. But the suffering caused by following the egoic mind eventually leads to our questioning the value and validity of our thoughts. Then the falseness of the "I" begins to be seen, the illusion of separation begins to dissolve, and we realize that there's something much more real and true to trust than the voice in our head.

TWO STATES

For the sake of simplicity, I like to speak of there being two states of consciousness: ego identification and being in Essence. One is a state where suffering is common, and the other is a state of no suffering. By suffering, I mean feeling uncomfortable, contracted, tense, confused, dissatisfied, unhappy, or caught in unpleasant emotions like anger, fear, sadness, guilt, blame, shame, resentment, regret, jealousy, and hatred.

This kind of suffering comes from believing our thoughts, specifically, the ones that come from the ego, which is most of the thoughts that run through our mind. This unhappy state is the egoic state of consciousness, and it's the state most people are commonly in. It reflects the human condition. The other state is the one that we are learning to live from. It's a state of no suffering, freedom, wisdom, peace, love, contentment, joy, and gratitude, which is what we experience whenever we're in touch with our true nature.

To move from the ego to Essence requires being very present to reality: being in the moment and in our senses rather than lost in thought, lost in our mental world. When we're in touch with reality, with the subtle drives and intuitions arising within us and with what life is bringing us through our senses, we are also in touch with our true nature. On the other hand, when we're absorbed in our thoughts about ourselves, our life, other people, what we want, what we like or don't like, the future, and the past, we're lost in the ego's world, in a virtual reality of sorts.

When we are identified with the egoic mind, we aren't being present to the moment, to reality, and we aren't in contact with Essence. Once we stop identifying with the voice in our head and give our attention to what we're actually experiencing in the here and now, we experience the natural peace, wisdom, love, joy, acceptance, and gratitude of our true nature.

Our thoughts often make it difficult to pay attention to reality because they grab our attention. Negative and fearful thoughts, in particular, seem especially important to pay attention to. Not paying attention to such thoughts seems unwise and unsafe, and thinking such thoughts makes us feel like we're doing something to keep ourselves safe. But if you examine this notion, you see that thinking doesn't have the power to stave off what we fear, nor do our thoughts have any ability to predict what's going to happen next.

We may think that paying attention to our fearful thoughts keeps us safe, but all thinking these thoughts does is take us out of reality, where we can be in touch with our inner wisdom, which *can* keep us safe. Instead of protecting us from what we fear, our fearful thoughts keep us stuck in the ego's reality, which is an unhappy reality, full of dissatisfaction, doubt, fear, and distrust.

If we persist in being involved with our egoic mind, it will be difficult to discover the truth about reality—that living in reality, instead of the ego's virtual reality, is a peaceful, safe, and joyous place and that within us is the wisdom and guidance we need to be happy and fulfilled. Being in the moment is where true happiness lies, but we won't discover that if we're wrapped up in the ego's world and believing the ego's perspective, which is one of fear and distrust.

Everyone knows what being in the moment, or being present, feels like. We all experience this many times a day whenever we're fully involved with, or absorbed in, whatever experience we're having rather than absorbed in our thoughts about that or something else. Being in the moment is an experience of being lost in what we're doing, as opposed to being lost in thought.

When we lose ourselves in what we're doing or in whatever is happening, what we lose is the sense of *me*. We are still experiencing, but the sense of "I" is no longer central to that experience; the sense of being someone who is experiencing something is absent. There's just experiencing. We aren't referring the experience we're having back to ourselves—to how it's going for *me* and what it means to *me*. When we lose ourselves this way, we enjoy whatever we're doing, regardless of what that may be. Being lost in the moment is inherently pleasurable and fun. Children do this naturally in their play. Play or fun could be defined as losing yourself in what you are doing.

Importantly, in addition to peace, enjoyment, fun, happiness, and love, being in the moment gives us access to Essence's guidance and wisdom. When we are in the moment, Essence can more easily guide us in playing our part in the Whole. The ego isn't in touch with the Whole's plan, and the ego's plans are often in conflict with that higher plan, although not always. Following the ego instead of Essence leads to lots of experiences and often some painful growth and not as much ease and fulfillment as following Essence.

LIVING THE LIFE YOU WERE MEANT TO LIVE

When I say there's a higher plan, I don't mean to imply that our lives are predetermined or that the specifics of that plan are spelled out before we are born, but that Essence, or our soul, has certain intentions for our life that take into account our individual evolution as well as the needs of the Whole.

There has to be a way for Essence to convey its intentions to us, and its way is not through the mind because the mind is generally already cluttered with ideas, beliefs, judgments, opinions, fears, desires, and other conditioning. The egoic mind has an agenda and a direction of its own that's often quite different from Essence's.

For Essence to reach us to guide us, it needs other avenues than the mind, although it *can* use the mind and does at times when the mind is clear and receptive. However, usually Essence uses the intuition and other signals to point us in directions it intends. When we follow these intuitions and signs, it feels right, and we feel elated, excited, and at peace. When we don't follow them, we often feel unhappy, lost, restless, even depressed.

The only thing that can interfere with noticing and following Essence's communications is a thought. What a surprise to realize this, when thoughts are generally so valued. Thinking is a precious thing—the ability to cognize, learn, read, and do all the other things our minds are capable of. But the nearly ceaseless stream of thoughts going on in our mind is not so precious, although we may believe it is and enjoy thinking these thoughts if we haven't examined or questioned them.

We aren't taught to observe our thoughts and question them, and we don't usually think of doing this unless spiritual teachers, therapists, or other healers suggest it.

We also aren't usually encouraged to pay attention to anything but our thoughts as possible guidance. Many of us assume there's nothing else to pay attention to, but is that true? We actually follow all sorts of intuitions and subtle cues all the time, often without realizing it. Everyone has some access to intuition, and Essence uses other things as well to steer and guide us, such as synchronicities, crises and other events, books, information on the internet, and words that come out of other people's mouths.

We are being guided to live the life we are meant to live, and this guidance shows up in various ways in each moment. If we're paying attention to our thoughts, we might very well miss these cues. The egoic mind offers guidance too and drives us with its desires. So we have a choice: We can follow the conditioning, drives, and desires of the ego or the more subtle cues of Essence that are coming out of the flow each moment. These two different ways of living and being can lead to quite different lives. Most people's lives are the result of a combination of following the egoic mind and following Essence.

So what might a life of following the egoic mind look like? That's easy to describe because such lives are very common, since most people are identified with their egoic mind much of the time. Most people allow their thoughts to determine what they believe and say and do. There's nothing wrong with this, since we learn and evolve as a result of whatever we experience.

But when we listen exclusively to our egoic mind, we are likely to make choices based on what we or others think we *should* do rather than on our deepest desires, the intentions of Essence.

A life based on following "should"s can still be valuable and productive, but it's unlikely to be very happy. "should"s are other people's ideas about what our life should look like, and how can others know this? Only we can know what's best for us to do. Only we know what will fulfill us and make us happy, and that's discovered by following our Heart—Essence—not our egoic mind, not "should"s. Essence communicates its plan to us moment by moment, primarily intuitively and also through inspiration and joy.

Let me give you an example from my own life about how important, but not necessarily easy, it is to follow the Heart. In my thirties, I was supported by my husband in an adequate lifestyle. I was looking for a job in the counseling field but unable to find one. He urged me to take a secretarial job because he thought I should be bringing in some income. I was miserable at this job, with phones constantly ringing and a high level of stress, something I don't do well with. I remember crying one day on my way home, just feeling fractured by the stress, noise, and busyness of that environment. My husband finally gave in and let me quit this job and stay home. What developed from staying home and not working was my writing career, which seems to be what I came here to do. It's certainly what I love doing—where my joy is. One way or another, life has continued to support me in this work.

The way I see this now is that life had provided me with a partner who was capable of and fairly willing to support me, while life had limited my opportunities for fulfilling employment. In this way, life—Essence—steered me into writing. Without such a perfectly designed situation, I probably wouldn't have had time to explore and develop this ability. I may have never even realized I had it. Sometimes life, through illness or other obstacles, makes room for us to discover a talent or something about ourselves that wouldn't have been discovered any other way.

Often the rightness of things isn't apparent until many years later, if even then. Nevertheless, when something is right, it *feels* right at the time, even though we may not know why. We can trust this. It's the way our Heart speaks to us. How often has life steered you in a direction you hadn't considered or that you initially thought you *shouldn't* go in, only to discover later the perfection of that direction? Our "should"s and other people's "should"s are often at odds with our higher plan.

People who are chronically unhappy, depressed, or caught in some kind of addiction are likely to be living a life that is out of step with their higher plan. It might be that they aren't doing work that suits them or they aren't using some talent they have. It might be that they're in a relationship that doesn't fit for them, one that limits their opportunities or ability to be who they want to be in the world or develop themselves in ways that are meaningful to them. We often make compromises or stop doing certain things we love doing for the people in our lives, not realizing how much we're hurting ourselves and the Whole by not pursuing our Heart's desire.

Sometimes in order to follow our Heart, change is necessary, and therein lies the rub for many people. Many aren't willing to change something because of certain beliefs they have or because they're too frightened to step out of a job or relationship that doesn't fit for them. It's too easy to believe our fears and not easy to listen to our Heart when it's prompting us to make a difficult change.

Many people never get beyond their doubts and fears, and they miss out on living the life they were meant to live. When that happens, the soul adjusts or keeps nudging them toward their deepest desires. The soul has all of eternity to experience what it needs to experience, and the Whole will adjust. But unfortunately, happiness and fulfillment are the price paid for believing doubts and fears instead of trusting the Heart. Not trusting the Heart results in a loss for the individual and for the Whole.

THE WORLD THE EGO CREATES

What happens when a majority of people in society follow their egos instead of their Hearts? Fortunately, even those who are very ego identified usually fulfill their higher plan, at least to some degree. If not, the Whole adjusts accordingly. Even those who are very ego identified respond to their Heart's nudges some of the time and so generally do find themselves in fields and activities that fit for them and provide some happiness and fulfillment.

Nevertheless, people who are ego-driven create a world that runs on the ego's values, a world that overvalues money, power, physical beauty, comfort, fame, success, and material possessions and undervalues the things that make our Heart soar: love and connection with others, growth, peace, creativity, nature, and contact with our spirit.

Our world is a world whose values are backwards, and yet if you ask people what's important to them, they'll list the values of the Heart. We are all in touch with our innate goodness, and yet we listen to our egoic minds, which prod us to go after more money, more things, more power, more worldly success—more and better of everything. The message we get from the media and corporations who are trying to sell us the things with which the ego is enthralled is that these are what make for happiness. But most of us have discovered that the things the media's trying to sell us don't make us happy, at least not for long.

We all long for a deeper connection with life, one that allows our love to flow and allows us to relax and be at peace once and for all. Everyone wants the same things—peace, love, happiness, and fulfillment. The ego has one way of trying to get these things, and our Heart knows another way. The Heart's way is very individual—what fulfills and makes one person happy isn't necessarily what fulfills another. Each of us has to find our own way to what fulfills us. Trusting life allows us to follow our Heart and create the life that will bring us happiness and fulfillment. It also allows us to drop into the moment, where "the peace that passeth all understanding" is always available.

CHAPTER 2
Why Trusting Life Isn't Easy

OUR DUAL NATURE AS EGO AND ESSENCE

Human beings don't trust life. Why? Because we have an ego, and egos are programmed to not trust life. Why? That's a deeper question and may not be entirely answerable. The answer, in part, is that the ego is an aspect of the human animal that keeps us safe, so it's always on the lookout for what *might* be dangerous or a threat to our safety. As a result, we notice movement, inconsistencies, differences, details, and the slightest changes in our environment, all in service to our safety. Our ego is there to watch our back. It thinks of everything that could go wrong. It assumes the worst and attempts to plan for it. This is valuable, of course. But the ego's viewpoint is narrow—"Life is dangerous!"—and the ego doesn't notice or acknowledge the other half of the truth: Life is supportive.

Isn't it interesting that we can even talk about the ego this objectively? It must not be who we really are. The ego and its perceptions must not be the whole story. What is it that is able to be aware of this aspect of our humanity and able to recognize that the ego's perceptions aren't necessarily the whole truth, or at least able to contemplate this possibility? Our mind has the capacity to reason, think, evaluate, and decide whether the ego's reactions to life are helpful or not, whether they even need to be paid attention to at a particular time. There's something else here that's aware of the dangers the ego perceives in the environment or in another person and concludes whether or not it's an actual threat. What is this that uses the mind but isn't the mind or the ego? What is it that is wise?

In addition to the ego's watchful eye, wisdom is here. Wisdom shows up in our body rather than in our mind, as an instantaneous knowing, or clarity, about something. We may put this knowing into words, but wisdom isn't the same thing as our thoughts about something. Wisdom is the ability to apply our knowledge and experience to a particular situation and act effectively. When we're faced with a problem, something uses the mind to search through memory banks for information, weigh the information and experience stored there, and balance that with our ego's reactions.

There's something else here that is living this life that is beyond the mind, beyond conditioning, beyond information, and beyond the ego, but it doesn't have a face or a personality. It's beyond the body, beyond gender, beyond roles, beyond personas or personality traits. It is the Silent Watcher, who acts and speaks through the body, who uses the ego and body-mind but is more than the sum of all of these parts.

The funny thing is that it seems like we are inside the body. And it seems like we are a male or female with a set of thoughts and other conditioning that seem to be our personal thoughts and conditioning. It seems like we are an individual with lots of fears, desires, beliefs, and doubts and questions about life and how to live it. Much of the time, we don't feel very wise, but confused and at the mercy of life and our thoughts, feelings, and desires.

And yet, when we're able to move beyond the smaller definitions we have of ourselves, we can sense and discover that we are much more than all of our fears, desires, beliefs, judgments, opinions, self-images, memories, fantasies, and other thoughts. There's something else here that is more real and yet less tangible, something that can't be put into words.

What is this that exists and is conscious beyond all your thoughts, all the problems you believe you have, all your fears and desires, all your images of the past and future, and all your self-images and roles? What is aware of and beyond all of these—because there is something, isn't there?

You can see why spiritual traditions have often referred to this great mystery of who we are as Emptiness, Nothingness, the Mystery, or the Nameless. Something exists that is you, but it isn't what you normally think of as yourself. It is given many other names, such as Essence, the true self, the higher self, the Self, the Silent Watcher, the Witness, the Divine, Source, Being, Silence, Presence, the soul, and Spirit. To be a little more precise, I use the term Essence to refer to the Divine, or the Oneness, as it manifests through an individual—as the God within us; while I use the term God, Oneness, or Source to refer to the godhead, or Creator.

So there is what we *think* of ourselves as and there is what we really are. We have a dual nature—the ego and Essence, the false self and the true self. What's odd is that we're programmed to believe we are who we *think* we are—the false self—and to overlook our true nature as Essence. We're programmed to believe we are something we're not!

This programming allows the Oneness to have the experience of being an individual (which it couldn't have as Oneness) and to have a unique experience through each of us, which is how the Oneness is exploring its own creation. This programming, as mentioned earlier, also provides the suffering that eventually wakes us up out of the nightmare of ego identification and motivates us to discover who we are and how to live as that in the world.

THE INSTINCTUAL EGO

An aspect of the ego is the instinctual self, which protects us by anticipating and being watchful for danger and threats. This aspect of the ego has a particular job and therefore a particular way of perceiving the world. Its job is to watch for and notice certain things, while disregarding other things. This watchfulness and cautiousness serve us to some extent and don't necessarily cause suffering if we are simply aware of our instinctual self's voice of caution and don't let it scare us. This aspect of the ego is activated when we enter a dark room, for instance. It cautions us: "Be careful! Go slowly. Don't trip."

The types of thoughts that belong to it are: "Watch out! You don't know what he might do next," "Look both ways before crossing this street," "Check the expiration date on this package of meat," "Better slow down around this corner."

The instinctual aspect of the ego doesn't generally cause us suffering because it simply warns us of immediate possible dangers based on instincts, experience, and stored knowledge. It doesn't personalize events or circumstances (e.g., "You're going to be in trouble now!" "That would be a really stupid move," "Don't forget to do that, like you always do"). It is objective and helpful and never demeaning, judgmental, harsh, or angry. However, its warnings aren't always needed nor do they reflect an actual danger, but only a potential one based on experience, knowledge, and the ego's tendency to expect problems or dangers.

There's another aspect of the ego, however, which is similar to this cautionary voice, but it speaks to us in a much more personal way, often like a parent or an authority figure. We'll call it the conditioned self or the voice of conditioning. This voice doesn't warn of immediate dangers but ones it believes might happen *in the future*, while the instinctual aspect of the ego warns of potential immediate threats based on current sensory input. The voice of conditioning paints a picture of a hypothetical future threat and cautions us about that, often in a way that makes us feel afraid. It creates fear by presenting us with a fearful future possibility, while the instinctual side of the ego doesn't make us feel afraid as much as cautious.

We have to ask: What is this future threat based on? Is it a true and accurate representation of what will happen if we do or do not do something? Does the conditioned self actually know the future? We'd have to conclude that it doesn't actually know what's going to happen, since that's what experience has shown us, although the conditioned self (our egoic mind) often sounds like it knows what it's talking about and may convince us as well.

More likely, the conditioned self's guesses about what's going to happen are based on some tragic incident in a movie we saw, something terrible that happened to someone we know, or something we read or heard about. Our minds are full of horrifying possibilities, especially these days, with all the negative news stories and violent TV shows and movies. It's no wonder most of us have a lot of fear, when we're exposed to every terrible thing that's happening and has ever happened on the planet along with every possible imagined horror.

Our mind stores not only what we've actually experienced, but also everything we see and hear, and all of this contributes to our view of the world. With the kind of input we're receiving from the media these days, we can't help but be fearful, probably more fearful than many humans before us who were not exposed to the violence and tragedy we see daily. As a result, we have an enhanced ability to imagine the worst, in graphic detail—as if we weren't already good at doing that!

Our imaginations are powerful! They create feelings, such as fear, and those feelings determine how we perceive and feel about life and what we do and don't do. Reading about or seeing terrible things is bound to make us feel afraid and somewhat powerless, just as experiencing such things does. Without being aware of it, by viewing violence and disasters, we are subtly being negatively programmed and traumatized. These negative images affect us more than we may realize. Images go right into the unconscious, where they are stored and affect us unconsciously. Those who unplug themselves from the media's barrage of negative images for any length of time discover how much easier it is to be happy and at peace. Being exposed to so much negativity and so many stories of tragedy isn't healthy emotionally or spiritually.

When we hear of or see so much pain and difficulty, it scares and saddens us. These images and the feelings they create can be demoralizing to the human spirit because they cause us to see the world as dangerous and to question whether a good life or happiness is even possible in such a world. They rob us of our trust and confidence in life, almost as much as if we experienced the events ourselves. What a different experience it is when we feel the opposite—that we are safe and anything is possible.

Alternately, violent images can harden and deaden us to the reality that they represent. This is especially true when children, who have a limited experience of reality, are bombarded with violent images. How can videos games, for instance, that allow children to practice killing and beheading people not have an effect on children?

What if you believed that this is a wonderful world, a paradise of abundance, love, and support? Contrast that with feeling like life is dangerous and hard and believing the world is going down the tubes, as many of the sci-fi movies (e.g., *Mad*

Max and *Water World*) portray life on this planet in the future. Our egos are already good at seeing problems, difficulties, and dangers. Watching such things depicted through the media reinforces the ego's view of life—its fear and distrust. The ego's perspective is strengthened by such images, which doesn't help us be at ease in life nor help to make this a better, more peaceful and loving world. Depicting or giving voice to the ego's fears only increases the ego's strength in the world.

Is that how you want to perceive life? We have a choice. Our ego's fearful perception of life doesn't match reality, although it can create a fearful reality to some extent—a reality full of fear. If we want a happier, more peaceful and loving reality for ourselves and the rest of humanity, we have to stop buying into the ego's perceptions, which create fear and negativity, and begin to see this beautiful world and its innately good people for what they are.

How you perceive the world is your choice, and your perceptions create your world to some extent, or at least your experience of it. You can see the world through your ego's eyes or the eyes of the Being that you really are. When you distrust and fear life, you're seeing life through the ego's eyes.

THE CONDITIONED SELF

Unlike the more instinctual side of the ego, the conditioned self actually has little value. The conditioned self is reflected in the egoic mind as the voice in our head. This voice at times appears to be our own voice and at other times to be someone else talking to us or even a dialogue between two voices. The proof that this mental chatter has little value is that there are many who no longer pay attention to this voice and no longer allow it to determine their speech, actions, or how they feel. These are the happiest people on the planet. They're considered awakened or enlightened, although to them this state of freedom from the egoic mind is very ordinary. We are all destined to live from this state, just as they do. It is our natural state.

Most people experience their natural state, or Essence, only occasionally and then usually only briefly. Those who have awakened out of the egoic state of consciousness are pointing the way to a new way of being in the world, one that will create a happier, more peaceful and loving planet. This way of being perceives all as valuable and precious and all as one. This is the truth about life. Our current way of being and the world it has created is the ego's way of being, and look what suffering it's caused and is causing and what a mess it's made of our beloved earth.

Our salvation from suffering and the salvation of humanity and the earth will come from learning to move beyond the egoic mind, which is a primitive and outdated aspect of our humanity. If humanity has ever needed the egoic mind, we don't need it now. What we need now more than anything is to see that we don't need to listen to our often destructive, unloving, fearful, limiting, and judgmental thoughts. Listening to them has gotten us into the mess we are in, but fortunately there's a way out. It's not that easy, but the alternative—to remain under the rule and at the mercy of the egoic mind—is a very unhappy and dysfunctional place.

The reason it's not that easy to move beyond the egoic mind is that the egoic mind captivates us through fear. Fear keeps us listening to the egoic mind, believing it, and doing its bidding. So what are we afraid of? One thing we're afraid of is our body being harmed or killed. That fear is part of our survival instinct, and it naturally arises whenever there's a threat or perceived threat. Fear that arises in response to something that's actually happening is natural and has no long-term effect on the way we perceive the world: When we're threatened, we experience fear, and then it's gone. This isn't the kind of fear we need to move beyond—and we won't. No matter how enlightened we are, if a car is barreling head-on toward us, for example, we are likely to be shot through with fear and adrenaline, and that's the appropriate reaction.

The fear that we can learn to move beyond is fear that comes from a thought—from the egoic mind, the conditioned self, not from the instinctual self. The egoic mind makes up things to be afraid of based on conditioning, past experiences, and what it's seen and heard. It makes them up! A scary thought appears in your mind, and you feel fear in your body. This physiological response, then, reinforces the made-up fear. The fear came from a thought—from your imagination—and then the body's response makes that thought seem true because the body responds equally to real and imagined fears. The body doesn't distinguish between the two. So what is being suggested is moving beyond *imagined* fears, that is, every *thought* that produces fear in the body.

There are real threats and imagined threats. An imagined threat is anything that isn't happening *now*. Imagined threats are made-up threats that seem like real possibilities. That's where the problem lies. Imagined threats seem really important to pay attention to—but are they and what happens if you do? First of all, how can an imagined threat be real? By definition, an imagined threat is imagined and not real. An imagined threat could be real only if there were a direct relationship between what we imagine and what becomes real in the future. And there isn't. What we imagine doesn't come to pass.

Let this sink in a moment, because we, as humans, seem to have deep programming to the contrary. We are programmed to believe the thoughts that run through our mind, and we're even programmed to believe our imaginations about the future. When it comes to dreams and fantasies, we'd like to believe that what we imagine will come true. Perhaps we think that if we realize the truth about our fears, we'll also have to realize the truth about our fantasies—that they're made up as well. In any event, neither our fears about the future nor our fantasies come true as we imagine them.

We give our thoughts much more power than they deserve. They motivate us and make us feel certain ways, but by themselves, our thoughts have no power. Unless we believe them, they have no power at all. Even if we believe our fears and fantasies, they still aren't meaningful by themselves. They are not a window into the future. They are made up. They aren't even made up by anything wise, but by the ego, the programmed aspect of ourselves that's run by fear, dissatisfaction, greed, power, and other base emotions. The ego is not the finer side of humanity, but the darker side.

It's a good thing we aren't our egos! But as long as the majority of people listen to the egoic mind, what we get is a world that's run by fear and shaped by activities driven by fear, such as war, accumulation of wealth, struggles for power, hoarding, mismanagement of human and natural resources, and a general disregard for life. We all need to discover what's really at the core of life and who we really are so that love can run the world instead of fear. Love would create a very different world, and we need this to happen now.

So what happens when we believe our imagined fears? We make different choices than we would otherwise. We create a different life than the one we would have created if we hadn't believed those fears. For example, if you're afraid no one will love you, then you might marry the first person who shows an interest in you or accept an abusive relationship rather than go it alone. Or if you're afraid you can't support yourself, you might seek a mate who can take care of you and miss out on developing your own talents and abilities or on meeting someone you'd be happier with. Or if you're afraid you won't make enough money doing what you'd like, you might take a job doing something you don't like just for the pay. Or if you're afraid of not being liked because you think you're not pretty enough, you might have plastic surgery and spend a lot of time at the gym and shopping for clothes instead of doing something more meaningful. Or your solution to your fear of not being liked might be to drive an expensive car or live in a fancy house. All of this catering to the ego's fears costs a lot of money, so now you really need that high-paying job—whether you like it or not! At this point, doing something less stressful or more to your liking or more meaningful doesn't even seem like an option (although it always is).

The ego can keep us very busy trying to assuage its fears. It created the rat race and it keeps us in that rat race. The ego drives us to get more of whatever it feels it needs to be happy, secure, and at peace. But no matter how much we get of what the ego wants, it's never enough because there's no end to the ego's fears.

The ego is in the business of generating fear—and desires. The ego's fears and desires go hand-in-hand: The ego desires the things it desires—money, possessions, status, success, power, security, comfort, pleasure—because it's afraid that without these, happiness and survival won't be possible. Its fear of not being happy and not being safe drive it to acquire the things it values and believes will make it happy and safe: lots of money, a beautiful house, a prestigious job, a fancy car, a younger face and body, and so on.

The ego knows of no other route to happiness, and it can't imagine feeling safe, secure, and happy without the things it desires. So the materialistic lifestyle is born, and we all know what that looks like and where it leads. One thing that makes trusting life difficult is that so many people in the world are believing their imagined fears and living accordingly—living a materialistic and superficial lifestyle, devoid of true meaning and connection with spirit. With all this fear-driven hustle and bustle going on around us, making a different choice can be challenging even once we've seen the folly of following the ego's desires and fears rather than listening to our Heart.

How Are Your Fears Shaping Your Life?

Take a moment and examine how fear might have driven or might be driving you and what you do with your time and energy. In what areas of your life have you made or are you making choices based on some fear? It's not that difficult to pinpoint where fear is influencing our choices because we're usually unhappy with the areas of life that fear is ruling. What fear or fears, if any, have driven you to make choices you're unhappy with? Fear of not having enough? Fear of not being good enough? Fear of not being loved? Fear of not being respected? Fear of not being special? Fear of not being safe or surviving? We all have these fears, but they don't have to determine your choices in life.

What fears come up most for you? Do any of them interfere with your functioning? With being joyful? How do you allow your fears to limit you? How much of your time goes to trying to prevent what you fear? Do your fears keep you from doing what you really want to do, what your Heart wants to do?

What else is there besides the lifestyle the ego creates? Where is the model for a healthy, happy, fulfilling lifestyle, one grounded in our true nature? Some people are living such a life, but they are bucking the dominant culture and the corporate media. One way to see our way clear from these influences is to align ourselves with others with more spiritual values and unplug as much as possible from those institutions, people, and media that help perpetuate egoic values. It's pretty hard to be participating in the rat race and not be affected by it.

THE EGO CAN'T CONTROL LIFE

The ego has a hard time trusting life because real life isn't the way the ego wants it to be; life—reality—is the way it is. One thing the ego doesn't like about life and one reason the ego doesn't trust life is that life is unpredictable and not under the ego's control. This unpredictability and lack of control make the ego feel vulnerable and life seem dangerous and untrustworthy.

Do unpredictability and lack of control make life untrustworthy? Some of the most wonderful things that happen to us are unexpected and outside our control: We suddenly meet someone and fall in love, we're surprised with an invitation to go somewhere we've always wanted to go, we unexpectedly get laid off and find an even better job. Not trusting life because we can't control it is like not trusting a smart car (i.e., a computer-driven car of the future) because you can't control it. Not being able to control life doesn't make it untrustworthy anymore than not being able to control a smart car makes a smart car untrustworthy. Something is in control of life that *is* trustworthy.

Since life isn't under the ego's control, sometimes things happen that the ego doesn't like, and then it feels unhappy, angry, persecuted, and betrayed by life; life is deemed untrustworthy. Only if life always brought the ego what it wanted would life seem trustworthy to the ego. But is this a valid measure of life's trustworthiness? It puts the ego at the center of the universe and assumes the ego's desires are central to our happiness and the good of the Whole, which they aren't. There's something bigger going on here than the ego's desires, but the ego sees life through its lens of desire. It's true that we can't trust life to always deliver what we want, but we *can* trust life to be the way it *is*—unpredictable, mysterious, ever-changing, and not under our control.

Can you trust that what life delivers is good, that it's what you and the Whole need, even if it isn't what your ego wants? The ego doesn't trust that. The ego's measure for good and bad is how closely something conforms to its desires and preferences. The ego's so sure of its opinions about life: "If I like it, it's good; if I don't like it, it's bad," as if the ego knows more about life than Life itself. The ego's opinions about life are based on the ego's likes and dislikes. Many other things—love, connectedness, exploration, discovery, creativity, learning, and growth—are undervalued by the ego. The ego doesn't want these more meaningful things more than it wants what it wants—but Life does!

Can you think of something that happened to you that you didn't like that turned out to be beneficial in ways you never imagined? One of the "worst" things that ever happened to me was my divorce, but it turned out to be a blessing because of the growth that came from it and the new life I created in California, which wouldn't have been possible otherwise. This ending wasn't the end of the world after all, although it seemed that way at the time. Life is wiser than we are. Our ego can't see the bigger picture, the greater design, which is always what we need, although maybe not what we wanted at the time.

Life loves love, connectedness, new experiences, exploration, discovery, creativity, learning, and growth. Life often brings experiences our ego might not like in order to teach and evolve us or move us on to something new, something that expands our understanding or talents and offers new opportunities. Some of the ways it does this is by preventing us from having what we want or by moving us out of the structures (e.g., a relationship, a job, a home, a city) our ego's choices have created. Life has its own agenda, and that agenda is often different from the ego's, which is based on desire-fulfillment and the ego's narrow perspective.

Life has higher purposes than desire-fulfillment, although Life is fine with allowing us to pursue our desires as long as they don't interfere with its higher purpose. We are here to do so much more than fulfill our ego's desires. Getting what the ego wants isn't particularly fulfilling. Life's agenda is more love-filled, creative, happy, and satisfying than getting what the ego wants. Not only is Life a wise teacher, but it's bringing us a life that's potentially full of love and meaning, although we might not realize this if we're railing against how Life is doing that.

Can you trust that life is not only bringing you what you need to grow and become a better human being, but also what you need to be truly happy and to fulfill a great plan? Life is carrying us forward toward greater wisdom, compassion, happiness, and fulfillment. The route is sometimes challenging, but those challenges are designed to steer and mold us in ways that benefit our soul's growth and those we may serve with the wisdom gained from those challenges.

THE EGO DOESN'T LIKE CHALLENGES

Another reason the ego doesn't trust life is that life is hard sometimes. Life is full of challenges the ego doesn't like, some that the ego itself created by choosing poorly or behaving badly, some that are part of our soul's plan, and some that are just part of being in a body. These challenges are not a reason to distrust life, however, because they are purposeful. Challenges teach and evolve us and develop certain qualities and traits, such as patience, responsibility, caution, compassion, and perseverance, that wouldn't be developed if our circumstances were always easy. Challenges make us better people if we can learn to handle them well and not become bitter, angry, or defeated.

This is just how it is on planet earth; challenges are part of life and part of having an ego. We can trust life to be full of challenges. Life is dependable that way. It was designed to be that way. We can't trust, or expect, life to be easy all the time. If we want or expect that, as the ego does, we'll feel angry, sad, betrayed, and persecuted by life. But life isn't persecuting us by bringing us challenges. They aren't proof of an unloving universe. We all have our share of them, and there's more wisdom and depth to be gained from them than we may realize. Our challenges were designed for us or created by our choices, and our task is to meet them with love and acceptance and grow from them.

THE EGO DOESN'T LIKE SUFFERING

Another reason the ego doesn't trust life is because there's so much suffering in life. But what causes this suffering? Is it life or how we relate to and think about life? Many spiritual teachings claim that suffering is optional and that it's possible to be in a state of peace regardless of our circumstances and the challenges we face. Being this free is, without question, very difficult; and yet it's still possible, as Viktor Frankl discovered after surviving imprisonment in a concentration camp during World War II. After this horrendous experience, he went on to become an important influence in the field of psychology, helping many find meaning and peace in life. His life story is a testament to the purposefulness of even our worst experiences, which doesn't, of course, excuse evil. I highly recommend his book *Man's Search for Meaning.*

Suffering, as I'm defining it, is created by the ego. Suffering is caused by how we think about a circumstance or an event, not by the particular circumstance or event. It's possible to experience very little suffering as we move through life, although few wouldn't suffer over life's more devastating experiences. For example, anyone would naturally grieve over the loss of a loved one or a home. However, many extend that grief unnecessarily by thinking about the loss long afterwards and by what they tell themselves about it: "It shouldn't have happened," "I'll never be happy again," "It's not fair," "I can't handle this," "No one will ever love me like that," "I can't manage by myself."

Suffering is an inside job—it's created by our mind. The ego generates the thoughts that cause us to suffer and then it suffers over the suffering it has created. The challenges in life aren't easy, but we don't have to suffer unnecessarily over them. By repeatedly bringing the memory of an unhappy event into the present moment and by telling stories about our experiences that make us feel bad, we create and maintain a negative feeling state.

The ego comes to negative and erroneous, or incomplete, conclusions about things that happen and suffers because of those conclusions. Then the ego blames life for that suffering. Did life cause the suffering or did the ego, with its angry and sad tales of woe and persecution?

For instance, let's say a friend didn't do something he said he would. What do you conclude? "I don't know why he didn't do it" would be about the only true conclusion you could come to. But the egoic mind is likely to jump to any number of conclusions in this and similar instances that result in negative emotions (suffering) and drama: "He doesn't care about me," "He's selfish," "He's irresponsible," "I've had it with him," "I'm never going to do anything for him again," "I'm never speaking to him again," "Something terrible must have happened!" Most people have egoic minds that like to stir up emotions and trouble, and yet, some manage to draw more neutral conclusions that don't cause them to suffer: "He must have gotten caught in traffic," "He'll probably do it another time," "It's okay if he forgot," "I'll just ask someone else to do it."

What we say to ourselves about our experiences really matters! What we conclude can make us suffer unnecessarily and create problems in our relationships or allow us to relax and feel loving. Anything we say to ourselves that puts us at ease with life drops us into Essence and gets us in touch with the wisdom and love at our core. We can experience negative emotions, drama, and suffering or love, peace, and wisdom. We are the master of our universe when it comes to our conclusions—we get to choose what to conclude about ourselves, other people, and life.

Unfortunately, most of us aren't aware of what we're concluding or that we even are concluding something. We assume our emotions and suffering are caused by something that happened or something someone said or did rather than something we said to ourselves.

We tell stories, and then we believe them. By stories, I mean we put a spin on something that happened. Instead of stating facts, such as "He didn't do it yet," we tell a story about it: "He didn't do it because...," "And that means...,""He always...," "He never...." We embellish the facts with our conclusions, assumptions, beliefs, judgments, opinions, or imaginations. We do this so automatically that we don't even realize we're doing it. It's what egos do, what we're programmed to do. And most of these stories make us feel bad. Life seems so difficult (so untrustworthy) when it's colored by these stories.

But there's something else here that's capable of noticing we're spinning stories and conclusions and capable of evaluating how true they are and whether or not doing this is a good idea. What is this that is objective, wise, and kind? I include "kind" because kindness is the natural result of being objective and wise, which are qualities of our natural state.

If we don't buy into the ego's stories and just stay in a place of having no conclusions and accepting that we don't really know what's true, we discover that there's something else here that can take the place of acting out of ego. It allows us to tell stories and suffer over them if we choose—it allows us to identify with the ego—but it would act differently if we tuned into it and let it move and speak through us.

Most of us live from the egoic state of consciousness because we aren't aware of another possibility, and we don't discover what else is possible until we stop listening to the ego's stories. Once we do stop, we experience the quiet wisdom and right action of our true nature. Until then, Essence is mostly in the background, waiting patiently for us to notice that something else is here, which is not a thing, but who we really are.

THE EGO TELLS STORIES

We get into trouble when we take things personally. What I mean by that, besides the usual meaning, is that we make ourselves unhappy when we personalize our experience, when we tell a story about our experience rather than just have the experience. Telling stories wouldn't be much of a problem if they were uplifting and true, but usually our stories are partial truths and complaints about life that generate unpleasant feelings. Those complaints and feelings color life and spoil the potential happiness and grace in each moment.

For example, you notice your spouse's clothes on the floor and say to yourself: "Those clothes were so expensive; I can't believe he/she threw them on the floor." That story can make you angry, and you might express that anger to your spouse or do something else in reaction to it (e.g., eat cake, go on a shopping spree, complain to a friend). Instead, if you're able to just notice the clothing and the story that arises, then anger and any other reactions the anger might spark won't happen. Then just pick up the clothes or don't pick up the clothes. End of story. The anger is unnecessary and so are the other reactions. Such feelings and reactions waste our energy and get us nothing but unhappiness. What if you just noticed what you notice without telling a story about it and then just responded? Voila! No suffering!

We create our experience of reality with the stories we tell about whatever we're experiencing. When we tell a positive story, we feel good; when we tell a negative story, we feel bad. Meanwhile, life is just the way it is, neither good nor bad (the clothes on the floor are just what they are, neither good nor bad). The egoic mind chooses to like or dislike something about every moment. The moment is the way it is, but the mind tells a story about it, judging or evaluating it, assigning meaning to it, and relating it back to the me: "This is good (or bad), and it means x for me."

These stories determine not only our experience of the moment and how we feel, but what we do next. The stories we tell often make us feel a certain way and react a certain way. So our stories are important: They determine our internal experience and often shape our behavior, which in turn, affects how others react to us. So reality is the way it is, and then we shape, or color, our experience of it with our stories, and that determines what happens next. When our stories are negative, usually the result of believing them is negative as well, and we suffer not only from the negative story, but from the consequences of believing that story.

When we just experience reality as it is, without putting our spin on it, life is much simpler and there's no suffering. Life is uncomplicated by unnecessary feelings and actions. So much of our doing is an attempt to fix our story or the unpleasant feelings (suffering) generated by that story. Without the story, we might not feel a certain way and we might not take action in a certain direction. Then what we would be left with is just the simple moment. And out of the simple moment come wisdom, clarity, and right action—action that is informed by our true nature rather than by the ego.

When we stop listening to the ego's stories, our true self—Essence—has room to move in our life. The Being that we are will move us to act and speak in ways that are most true and fulfilling for us and for the Whole. So rather than speaking the ego's words and following the ego's dictates, when we stop believing and responding to our mind's stories, we can begin to live from Essence.

The place of Essence is an impersonal yet intimate place. It's a place where we intimately experience life without personalizing what we're experiencing—we don't turn it into a story about *me*. When we're identified with the ego, we relate our experiences back to the *me*, to how the *me* likes or feels about the experience or how that experience might affect the *me*. We have an experience and instantly evaluate it: "Do I like it? Will it be good for me or not?" This personalization of experience is actually how the sense of *me*—the ego—is created and maintained.

The egoic self, the false self, is made up of ideas about what we like and don't like, what we believe and don't believe, what we want and don't want. When these ideas get tangled up with reality, that is, when they get inserted into reality, they change our experience of reality. The experience of reality without all this referencing to the *me*, is pure, simple, and uncomplicated. There's much less to do and no feelings to fix. What we're left with is pure being, simple experiencing, with no *me* experiencing it and having an opinion about the experience. Action might happen, but it happens spontaneously and easily, with little thought and no thought about *me*, what *I* like or don't like, what *I* want or don't want, just acting because it feels right to take action. Who knows why and who knows what that action will lead to—and we don't need to know.

This place of no *me* and pure being is a place of freedom, happiness, and contentment. The place where nothing feels personal is very free and pleasant because it's free from the constant self-referencing of the ego, which is an unhappy, contracted state—a place of suffering.

BEING PRESENT IS ABSENT OF SUFFERING

Terrible things do happen, and the suffering can be immense. And yet, some suffer less than others because of their state of mind—how much they're thinking and what they're thinking at the time. In a crisis, usually the more people think, the more they suffer, because their thoughts frighten them. Those who are very present to a life-threatening experience instead of caught up in their fearful thoughts often report feeling very alive and in touch with an inner strength that sustains them and helps them respond in appropriate ways. These individuals are often the ones who are able to save themselves and others. A power takes over and works through them that's beyond the mind and ego and simply acts wisely.

This same capacity for aliveness and being present in the moment instead of lost in our thoughts enables us to go about our ordinary life without suffering. Being present is a very different state of consciousness than the egoic state of consciousness, which is an experience of being in our head instead of our body and senses, of being absorbed in a mental world rather than in life as it's showing up right *now*.

Being lost in our mental world isn't a particularly pleasant way to go through life, but it seems to be our default position as human beings. We tend to be oriented toward thinking about life more than being present to it, or fully in it. Most people have one foot in real life, while the rest of them is lost in the clouds—thoughts. This is, to a large extent, the cause of suffering, because our thoughts reflect the ego's perspective, and that perspective is commonly one of fear, distrust, and discontentment. Being lost in our thoughts also means we aren't fully in touch with the beauty, peace, love, and gratitude of our natural state, which we experience when we are present to real life.

The ego is oriented toward the past and future, not the present. The ego often thinks about the past and future, although it also thinks about the present, which isn't at all the same as *being* present. The ego rejects life the way it is and turns away from it because when we do accept and experience life the way it is without all of our thoughts, the ego—the sense of *me*—disappears! We lose ourselves in the moment. When we, for once, stop thinking and let ourselves be fully involved in whatever's going on right in front of us and within us (i.e., sensations, intuitions, inner drives, inspiration, insights), we can't help but experience the Being that we are, because that is what's here and been experiencing life all along, although it's usually obscured by so much thinking.

We think ourselves into existence, and then we believe we are the ideas we have of ourselves. We create an internal image of ourselves made up of all the beliefs and ideas we have about ourselves: "I'm a mother," "I'm smart," "I'm old," "I'm friendly," "I'm weak," "I'm cute," "I'm competent," "I'm impatient," "I'm funny," "I'm fat," "I'm selfish." We believe that this self-image is what's living this life—but it isn't. How can an image do anything?

That image of who we are—the false self—is what interferes with experiencing who we really are. *Thoughts* are the only thing in the way of experiencing the Being that we are! They're the only thing in the way of experiencing Essence and enjoying life, since the experience of Essence is an experience of joy and love of life.

There is no suffering when we have both feet in the present moment reality, when we are fully in the here and now. Suffering only happens in response to a thought. Nevertheless, the mind loves to think about the past and future. We're programmed to love our thoughts, give them our attention, and believe they have some reality. But the truth is, the past and future are just thoughts—memories and imaginations. And these thoughts are often a source of suffering not only because of their content, but also because thinking divorces us from the *experience* of reality, which is inherently rich, vibrant, and alive.

How is it possible to suffer in the present? It's only possible if we bring thoughts into the present moment that cause us to suffer, such as "I wish I didn't have to do this now!" "I hate it when it's this cold!" "How am I ever going to get all this work done?" "Why can't I ever do this right?" We bring our judgments, desires, and negative stories into the present moment, and they make the moment unpleasant. They color it and determine our experience of it. Without such thoughts, there would be no suffering, just whatever experience we're having—plain and simple.

We suffer because we define our experience as bad. We focus on what we don't like about it or we make up a story about it that makes us feel bad. When we reject the experience we're having, we suffer; when we don't, we don't suffer. You could say that the definition of suffering is saying no to whatever we're experiencing, because these two things—

rejection and suffering—are so closely linked. When we aren't saying no to our experience, we don't suffer. The "no" causes the suffering, not the experience. The "no" is the negative story we bring into the experience that causes us to have a bad experience. This is why acceptance is emphasized so much in spiritual teachings.

The ego actually enjoys suffering. If this weren't the case, we wouldn't find ourselves stuck in suffering so much. A part of us likes to suffer! The ego causes us to suffer by saying no to what's happening and what's already happened, even though doing so is completely irrational, since it doesn't change anything.

All this rejection and the suffering created by that serves the ego: Rejecting, judging, and complaining about life keep us in a state of dissatisfaction and keep the ego in business. If we were to accept what is, we would drop into Essence, and the ego—the sense of *me*—would disappear. The ego doesn't want that to happen, so it keeps us busy with thoughts that create suffering, thoughts of dissatisfaction, in hopes that we'll look to it for solutions, which it readily offers. The ego creates the problem (suffering) and then offers solutions. This is how the ego maintains itself and keeps us tied to our thoughts and enmeshed in the egoic state of consciousness.

Many would argue that it's impossible to accept certain experiences because they're so terrible. There certainly are terrible experiences, and no one is suggesting you like them but simply that you accept that something you don't like happened or is happening. Suffering comes from fighting with or denying reality instead of accepting what already is the case.

If something is already the case, like your best friend is in the hospital on life support or your spouse has left, then believing, "This shouldn't be happening" or "This shouldn't have happened" will make you suffer unnecessarily, because anytime we argue with reality and believe a lie, we suffer. Suffering is how Life shows us we're believing something that isn't true: When we believe the ego's lies and stories (e.g., "This shouldn't be happening"), we suffer; when we accept that reality is showing up the way it is, we experience the peace and wisdom of our true nature. Life has a built-in correction mechanism.

The ego's world is a world of pain caused largely by believing lies or half-truths about life, ourselves, and others: "I never do anything right," "He doesn't like me," "She's never nice," "There's no point to life," "I'm not smart enough," "Life is unfair," "No one pays attention to me." When we believe these lies and half-truths, we suffer: We feel contracted, ill at ease with life, defeated. The ego is in the business of manufacturing lies, so when we're in its grip we suffer a lot. When, instead, we acknowledge what is true and accept that and don't tell stories about it, we are free to simply experience life as it is. And life as it is, is very beautiful, even when it's painful.

How bad can this moment be? If you don't bring a story into this moment about what you're afraid will happen, what you're unhappy about, or what you don't like, how bad can this moment be? Many years ago, on the day I was to have major surgery, I discovered this truth. I was dreading the experience and wondering how I would get through it, and then I realized that all I had to do was get through this moment... and this one... and this one. Taking it one moment at a time was easy! What was so bad about talking to the nurse? What was so bad about being taken in a wheelchair to the operating room? What was so bad about lying on the operating table? What was so bad about being given anesthesia? What was so bad about waking up in a hospital bed with my husband bending over me, smiling?

Being present in the moment is primarily a sensory experience and an experience of being conscious and of existing and also of naturally and spontaneously responding to life. You might feel moved to do something, and you do it, so then you experience that. Someone might say something to you, so then you experience that, and you might find yourself responding to that. Life is simpler than we think!–or simpler than *when we think!*

In this way, Life unfolds, one experience changing into another, all the while you are the Experiencer, who also responds to and interacts with life. The Experiencer is a co-creator with life, not just an observer of life. You are what experiences and co-creates with life as it is showing up in your now. All you have is now. What is showing up now? That is what's real. That is real life, not your preferences and dreams, but life stripped bare of these and the personal spin your ego puts on life.

HOW CHILDHOOD EXPERIENCES DAMAGE TRUST

We all have an ego that naturally distrusts life, but some people's egoic minds are more negative and distrusting than others. For them, trust is an issue that deeply colors their existence and often limits their potential for happiness. This distrust has usually been caused by childhood experiences. Emotional, sexual, and physical abuse and neglect are the most obvious circumstances that undermine trust. But a number of other things can also affect a child's trust in himself or herself, others, and life, such as a difficult birth, a traumatic injury, illness, surgery, a family crisis, a divorce, the death of or a serious injury to a parent, poverty, or even an unstable or a busy household or inconsistencies in parenting.

When we are growing up, we draw conclusions, some conscious and some unconscious, about ourselves, others, and life that affect how we see and respond to the world thereafter. Difficult experiences in childhood usually result in negative and limiting conclusions, while good experiences and nurturing parents results in confidence, good self-esteem, and trust in ourselves, others, and life.

Some of our most insidious conclusions are unconscious, and we may have to do some inquiry or psychotherapy to uncover them. But many of our limiting conclusions are ones we're already aware of, at least to some extent, and so are the people close to us. When we're afraid to try new things or we lack the confidence to pursue what we're good at and enjoy doing, then limiting beliefs are bound to be the cause. Once we uncover and fully investigate these limiting conclusions, they lose their power to restrict us, and we're more able to move beyond them.

Children are naturally not as skillful as adults at handling the world. As smart as a child might be, all children have to learn to use their bodies and minds and to communicate, and all this learning involves making a lot of mistakes. As a result of their having to be dependent on others and having to learn so much, children can easily feel inferior just because they are children.

Furthermore, because children are dependent on their parents, they tend to blame themselves and feel inferior if they have an unhappy childhood. If a parent is unhappy with them or even just unhappy in general, children tend to blame themselves for that. And when children are abused or neglected or unsupported, even in small ways, they blame themselves and develop a self-image of being unworthy, inferior, and unlovable. It would be too threatening to see their parents, whom they are dependent upon, as flawed, bad, undependable, or wrong. Children need these flawed, unhappy, and often angry and mean parents to take care of them. It's safer to see themselves as wrong or inferior.

So children tend to blame themselves for their unhappy childhoods, although most aren't conscious of doing this. They come out of childhood feeling bad about themselves (not trusting themselves) and bad about others and about life (not trusting others and life). They come to conclusions: "I will never be happy" (I can't trust life or me to bring me happiness), "I have to go it alone and take care of myself" (I can't trust others to take care of me), "The world is a scary place" (I can't trust the world), "Life is hard" (I can't trust life to be good or my life to turn out well).

Such conclusions are limiting because they often stop us from doing what we might naturally do to create a happy life. They also take the joy out of life moment to moment because they involve us with fears and a negative self-image that seems to need fixing. We see ourselves as someone with a problem, someone who is flawed or inferior and has to work hard to overcome that. And we see life as something to be feared, something that is against us.

These negative beliefs keep us locked into the egoic state of consciousness, which is a place of fear, dissatisfaction, and never being or having enough. Healing is often necessary before we're able to see that we are victims of our own thoughts, beliefs, and self-images and that these maintain and re-create the experience of life we had as a child. If, as a child, we were used to feeling bad about ourselves, afraid, powerless, and on edge, then there's a certain familiarity about this state that feels right and comfortable. Feeling good, happy, confident, and trusting can actually feel uncomfortable.

People who had difficult childhoods need to become comfortable with feeling good. They need to learn that it's okay and safe to be happy, confident, and trusting. They need to become familiar with the state of consciousness that is at peace with life and able to be relaxed and happy, a state of consciousness that those with happier upbringings take for granted and naturally live from, at least some of the time. Psychotherapy and other forms of healing work are usually needed to help those who had their trust damaged in childhood move into a new relationship with life, one that is more trusting. The role of a therapist is to be the positive parent and provide the supportive and safe environment that the person didn't have so that he or she can begin to experience what it's like to feel good about himself or herself and begin to trust life.

We also distrust simply because people around us distrust. So even if our childhood was generally supportive and loving, we pick up on any distrust our parents might have had, either just because they have egos and were caught in that state of consciousness a lot or because they had a childhood that taught them to distrust. As children, we learn from those around us, and if they were distrusting, then that becomes our conditioning as well.

Unfortunately, since most people live in the egoic state of consciousness most of the time, and this state is dominated by fear, trusting life seems out of step with most people and therefore wrong. So even if someone's trust hasn't been damaged in childhood, being trusting still isn't so easy when the world at large doesn't trust life. The beautiful connection with spirit that children who haven't lost their trust naturally have is weakened by encounters with the world of people who are afraid and distrustful of life.

We have to find our way back to this innocence because it's actually our natural and true state and what will make this a better world for everyone. It isn't airy-fairy to trust life, although it seems like that to the ego. Trusting life belongs to a state of consciousness that we all need to rediscover if we're to bring more peace and love back into the world, which has been overcome with fear and the violence that comes from fear.

RELIGIOUS TEACHINGS THAT DAMAGE TRUST

I met someone who explained to me that his religion had taught him the opposite of what I'm teaching, and that he'd come to see that the teachings he'd received didn't serve him or life. He was taught that, because he (and everyone else) was born sinful, he couldn't trust himself to be good and do the right thing. He was taught that he needed his religion and others in authority to tell him what to believe and how to behave, and if he didn't adhere to what they taught, he'd be damned for eternity. He was taught to believe, trust, and not question those who claimed to know the truth. The penalty for not believing or for even questioning what they taught was quite frightening. What's a child to do when faced with this?

It takes extraordinary courage to examine our beliefs when we're told they are inviolate. So many people never do, and certainly few children do. Those who taught this individual were taught the same thing, and so these beliefs get passed down from one generation to the next, with everyone being afraid to question what they've been told. This is a form of conditioning—religious conditioning—and fear keeps it in place, as is true of a lot of our conditioning.

Although there is value in religious and moral training, unfortunately this individual was taught to not trust his Heart. This is the antithesis of what's needed to live in alignment with spiritual principles. The Heart is our connection to the

Divine, and the Heart holds the truth about how to move in the world. Following our Heart is quintessentially moral.

The proof that the Heart is trustworthy is in where trusting the Heart leads. It doesn't lead to killing or harming others or to other acts we as humans generally agree are immoral, but to peace, acceptance, tolerance, love, compassion, happiness, and fulfillment of our life purpose. On the other hand, a great deal of harm has been caused by adhering to certain beliefs that have been passed down to us (i.e., conditioning), including racial prejudices and some religious beliefs.

Beliefs have been used to justify all kinds of hateful acts and divisiveness. The believers trusted that their beliefs were true and righteous, even though the results were hateful and went against all that we know in our Hearts to be right. They put their trust in the wrong thing. Beliefs too often do not reflect the Heart's, or Essence's, truth but the ego's because beliefs are conditioning; they're ideas passed down to us, sometimes by ignorant people whom we trusted because we didn't know better, not a deeper knowing of the truth. Beliefs are often just, plain false, while the Heart knows the truth. If it weren't for the Heart, we wouldn't be able to find our way out of the ego's lies to the truth.

What a backwards message this is—that we can't trust ourselves to know what's morally right or right in a particular circumstance and that we should trust someone else instead just because they say so. Did we not come from God, and do we not have a spark of divinity within us? I know I do because I experience it, and I trust my own experience of the Divine within me. This isn't a belief I have, but an experience of my own connection with the Divine. And I'm sure you feel it too.

The idea that we can't trust ourselves follows from the *belief* that human beings are innately bad and sinful and that they have to be taught to be good and dissuaded from being bad through punishment. Is it true that evil is our true nature? It's important to investigate and answer this question for yourself, because the answer determines whether you believe you can trust yourself—your Heart—or not, or whether you even believe you have a Heart.

Not everyone is in touch with their Heart, but everyone does have a Heart that speaks to them, and when questioned about the Heart, most know what's meant by that. The Heart is our inner guidance system, our connection with divine guidance. When we aren't in touch with our Heart or don't listen to it, we lose our way and get caught up in the ego's way, which is the way of selfishness, not love.

The ego is behind all unloving acts—all evil—because the ego is out for itself. It doesn't know how to love. It isn't the part of us that loves. Listening to the egoic mind and other people's egoic minds is the danger, not listening to our Heart. The ego is driven toward fulfilling its desires and drives, and the only thing preventing it from pursuing its desires at all costs is a connection to the Heart, which takes into consideration the good of the Whole and which is ruled by love.

If there is a Devil, or a cause of evil, it is the ego. We all have the capacity to do and speak evil because we all have an ego. But we are not our ego. Our true nature isn't evil, and that's the great, great, good news and why life is trustworthy—because goodness is at our core and at the core of everything else.

We don't need religion to teach us to be good or make us feel bad about hurting others. The proof is that there are many people who didn't grow up with religious training or who've eschewed religion who still live moral lives and feel bad when they hurt others. Most people have little trouble identifying what is good and what is evil, regardless of whether or not they've had religious training. Religious training or the lack of it isn't what determines who behaves well and who doesn't. Religious and non-religious people alike perform good acts and bad acts. There's something else that causes us to be good, or to at least strive to be good, that has little to do with religious training.

Those who do violence or harm in this world and who seem to feel no remorse aren't the norm for humanity. Those who do such things have usually been abused or damaged in some other way in childhood. There are often also metaphysical reasons for such evils. What is really going on when people commit a hateful act is not that they are expressing their inherently evil nature, but that they're responding unconsciously to their negative conditioning, their erroneous beliefs that result in negative emotions, like anger, sadness, fear, jealousy, resentment, shame, and hatred. Such individuals believe the prejudices and other lies they've been taught or the negative conclusions they came to as a result of being abused or unloved. The strong, negative emotions that follow from these beliefs often compel them to act in harmful ways.

When people stop believing the untrue beliefs and conclusions—the conditioning—that cause them to feel angry, sad, afraid, shameful, resentful, jealous, and hateful, they naturally respond to others with compassion, love, and acceptance. Our true nature, which is kind, shines through once the erroneous and negative beliefs have been seen through and we stop creating the painful emotions that fuel hurtful behavior.

Religions point to goodness and love as the highest values, but when religions fail to teach that we are innately good and that our negative thoughts and conditioning are the cause of evil, such religions may actually be contributing to the negativity in the world rather than lessening it, as they surely intend. Believing we are innately bad doesn't make us kinder and more loving but keeps us stuck in the ego, a place of shame and unworthiness. Just test this out for yourself: When you feel bad about yourself, how does that affect how you are in life? How about when you feel good about yourself? Doesn't that inspire you to be more loving, trusting, exuberant, and courageous?

Feeling good about ourselves and about life can only be a good thing. We need beliefs that help us feel good about ourselves, others, and life, not the opposite. Anything that does the opposite is anti-life and anti-love. Religions were founded on love, but many of the beliefs they teach result in the opposite of love. Such beliefs need to be questioned, as the value and truth of any belief is whether it takes us closer to love or farther away.

Another religious belief that interferes with trust is the idea that God is wrathful, vengeful, and punishing. This image of God is tied to the idea that we were born bad and can't be trusted to be good. If that's the case, then it makes sense that we would need a strict and harsh God to oversee us and make sure we behave and that we would need punishment to keep us in line.

This is a very bleak picture of humanity, and if we believe it, we aren't going to feel very good about ourselves, God, or life. Can feeling this way possibly be good for us or good for life? Is believing in this kind of God—is being God-fearing— what makes us good? If the difficulties in life are seen as punishment from God and we are seen as deserving such punishment, it's no wonder we're full of fear and distrust. Is fear a good thing?

This way of seeing God elevates punishment to something noble, necessary, and right, and I would argue that harshness and punishment create the very evil they're trying to prevent. We learn love by being loved. We learn violence by experiencing *and seeing* violence. We don't learn anything of value by being punished. Instead, we learn that we're bad, worthless, and unlovable. Love and goodness never came from feeling bad about ourselves. If we believe in a God that relates to us harshly, how does that affect how we see the world and how we are in the world? This is a belief that reinforces fear, which is the opposite of love. Fear is the ego's domain, not the Heart's.

Fortunately, we are innately good, so those who've been inculcated with this very negative image of God can still experience the goodness within themselves. They still have the capacity to know the truth—that love is behind all life, not cruelty.

In summary, trusting life isn't easy because...

- *We trust the ego (our egoic mind), and the ego doesn't trust life.*

- *The ego creates a lot of fear by imagining fearful future possibilities.*

- *Life doesn't conform to what the ego wants and doesn't want, and the ego can't make it conform.*

- *Life has challenges, and the ego doesn't like challenges, feels persecuted by them, and doesn't appreciate the value in them.*

- *The ego doesn't like suffering and blames life for the suffering, when the ego is actually the cause of suffering.*

- *Abusive, traumatic, and other challenging experiences, or even relatively minor lapses in support early in life can cause children to conclude that they can't trust themselves, life, or others.*

- *We live in a world where people are generally run by fear and don't trust life. We are influenced by the perceptions of those around us who don't trust life.*

- *Some religious teachings teach that we are inherently bad, and so we don't trust ourselves and we don't learn to trust our Heart. We won't discover how trustworthy life is if we are trusting erroneous beliefs, fear, and the egoic mind instead of the Heart, which is our divine guidance system.*

- *Some religious teachings portray God as something to be feared. How can life be trusted if God can't be trusted and God rules with fear?*

CHAPTER 3
Evidence That Life Is Trustworthy

LIFE IS CONSISTENT BUT NOT PREDICTABLE

It seems that whatever is behind life would determine if life is trustworthy. If evil were behind life, then life would be hard to trust, and we'd be wise not to trust it. On the other hand, if love and goodness are behind life, it would seem that life could be trusted. Isn't love what makes a parent trustworthy to a child? A parent who is unkind isn't trustworthy, while one who is kind is. Other qualities are crucial to trust as well, like consistency.

Consistency contributes to something's trustworthiness. Is life consistent? Life is full of changes, but life consistently changes—it can be trusted to change a lot. Is life consistent in other ways? The physical laws that govern this world are consistent and behave consistently. Gravity is consistently here, and the earth spins consistently on its axis and circles consistently around the sun. The colors we see are the same ones we're used to seeing—we don't suddenly see colors we've never seen before. Our bodies don't change into something else—we remain human throughout our lives. We all become older, not younger, and everything eventually dies. The sky remains above us and the ground below us. There is definitely something consistent about life. Life is consistently the way it is. In that, life is trustworthy.

One thing that can make life seem untrustworthy is that people can be inconsistent. When parents, for instance, are inconsistently available or respond inconsistently to a child, they're experienced as untrustworthy, and the child may conclude that life is also untrustworthy. It's a simple misunderstanding on the child's part to assume that life is untrustworthy when it is a parent who is, although it's natural for a child to make that assumption. Consistently available parents and consistent parenting are very important in establishing a sense of trust within a child, not only trust in the parents, but trust in life and in other people. When consistency isn't part of a child's home life, the child concludes, albeit falsely, that life and people in general can't be trusted.

Although people are free to behave however they choose, most people's behavior follows established rules, morals, and other conditioning and so is fairly consistent and therefore trustworthy. However, some people, especially those with mental illness or criminal tendencies don't follow society's rules or their Heart. Something else runs them that makes them act irrationally, erratically, unconventionally, and sometimes immorally, and that makes them untrustworthy. Most child abuse is perpetrated by those who are mentally ill, and children involved with such individuals are naturally left with a skewed view of humanity. Because of some of the mentally ill and "bad apples," people may seem more untrustworthy than they actually are.

Something else that can make life seem untrustworthy is that we don't know what's going to happen next. Life is unpredictable. It's a pretty safe bet that tomorrow the sun will come up and we'll get up and have the usual breakfast, but we never really know. Things related to our human existence, our life story, aren't very predictable because we have free will and because our lives have a trajectory that isn't known to us. Is that trajectory actually unknown and unpredictable just because *we* can't predict it? Maybe not. Maybe the direction of our life is only unpredictable from our perspective. Some people are able to predict things that would normally be unpredictable.

What if what's unpredictable to us and therefore seems untrustworthy isn't unpredictable from some other perspective and therefore is *not* untrustworthy? Just because we may not be aware of a greater design doesn't mean there isn't one or that it isn't trustworthy. What if there's a higher Intelligence that is consistent and loving, and it has a design for us and the Whole? What if it *is* us and the Whole? What if there's a higher plan in place for our life that moves us to shape our life in a particular way, and our free will operates within that greater design?

We appear to have free will, but it operates within certain boundaries; outside those boundaries, we aren't free to choose. We're free to choose things like what clothes to put on and what to have for dinner, but we aren't free to choose our race or gender. We didn't choose what country or family we were born in or how intelligent we are or what talents we have. These were chosen for us, in a sense. By what? That is the great mystery.

In any event, each of us has been given certain things to work with: We were born with a certain appearance, in a certain environment, and with certain talents and personality traits. This is the raw material we were given, which we didn't choose. Free will operates within the boundaries created by these things. If we have artistic talents, we probably won't choose to go into business. If we are introverted, we probably won't choose to become an entertainer. If we were born in poverty in India, we may not have the choice to go to college.

The environment and the opportunities and limitations it offers, and the personality traits and talents we were given determine to a large extent our destiny—what will happen in our life story. Knowing these things gives us some ability to predict our future, although only in a very general sense, and even then, not necessarily accurately. So much more shapes what will happen in our life story, including our free will and that of others and our capacity to move beyond any limiting psychological issues or beliefs that may create further boundaries.

But there's something else that inwardly pushes us in certain directions and not others, something that inspires us to do something, say something, or pursue a particular path. What is that? Is that our free will or something else? Is free will the ego's will or something else—or both? When we begin to examine the mystery at the core of life, it just seems to get more mysterious.

We may never know for sure what is behind life, at least while we are still in the body. Nevertheless, what we believe about life and about what's behind it is very important. It determines the lens through which we look, what we see, what we don't see, how we behave, how we feel, how we respond, and what comes back to us. And because our beliefs determine all those things, they also determine our destiny or, rather, to what extent we'll fulfill our destiny, or the plan for our life, the role we came to play in the Whole.

The unpredictability of our life story is necessary to our life plan. The fact that we can't predict what will happen next in our life isn't a sign of life being untrustworthy, but an indication of a higher plan at work that requires unpredictability.

These two things—unpredictability and a plan—may seem contradictory, but if our life plan were known to us and therefore predictable, we wouldn't have the experience of free will and all the growth that comes with that. We'd just be acting out a predetermined script and not making choices or responding spontaneously to what life brings. Free will allows us—the Divine through us—to freely explore and evolve from those choices. And that is part of the plan.

The Divine is having a unique experience through each of us, and it can only do so if we aren't aware that we are the Divine but we believe we are a particular individual. The Divine wants to experience certain things through us, and it can't have the experience it intends if it already knows the plot. It wants to get lost in the story it's living out and play it out without knowing what will happen next.

Not knowing what's ahead makes the story interesting, like not knowing how a movie or novel will end. Life feels interesting, exciting, and adventuresome when we don't know what's going to happen next. If we were to know, what would be the point of life?

The Divine not only wants to have lots of experiences, but it has a higher plan in which these experiences play a part. The Divine is having an individual experience through each of us, and that individual experience is also meaningful to the Whole. So there's a higher plan for each individual and a higher plan for the Whole *and* a playing out of these plans blind, without knowing where it all will lead, which makes life very interesting and mysterious. Everyone loves a mystery!

JOY AND LOVE POINT THE WAY

There *is* a plan (you get to choose whether you believe that or not), but it isn't a given that we'll fulfill it or fulfill it in a way that was intended. What can interfere with that plan are our beliefs—about ourselves, others, and life. Our beliefs are often limiting because most of them come from the ego and take us in the ego's direction instead of Essence's, or the higher plan's. Without our beliefs, we can find our way much more easily to where we're meant to go.

Isn't it ironic that beliefs, which seem so true and valuable, are actually what can be most limiting? This is because most beliefs aren't actually very true (or not the whole truth anyway) because beliefs are just conditioning. Conditioning is useful, but it doesn't hold the key to how to live your life or fulfill your destiny. Conditioning is meant to help us function, and some of it does that, but much of it just gets in the way of living life as the beautiful Being that we are. Many of our beliefs get in the way of being happy, which hopefully we can all agree is a worthwhile goal.

We all have a lot of false and useless conditioning. Our conditioning makes us think of ourselves in certain ways that can be limiting: "I'm not smart enough to succeed at that," "My mother would have a fit if I became an artist," "Girls can't do science," "Making money is more important than doing what you want to do," "You should carry on the family business." We have so many ideas about what we should do and what our life should look like, but are they true, and where did they come from? Is the source of these ideas trustworthy? What are we trusting when we trust our ideas? What happens when your ideas are in conflict with another sense of what seems true—with your Heart, with what you'd *love* to do? Then, what do you trust? What is more trustworthy?

People suffer when their ideas—their conditioning—are at odds with their Heart. This conflict can feel almost life threatening because often these ideas are ones we received from people we care about and are or were dependent on, from parents and others close to us. To not agree with these ideas feels like disagreeing with the truth, with the voice of God, with what's right, with your parents!

Such ideas are not necessarily the truth even though others believe they are and questioning them feels dangerous. They are just what others believe and taught us and what we picked up along the way. They aren't tailor-made for us. They are one-size-fits-all: They are supposed to fit everyone, but they don't. And they certainly don't fit all occasions. When ideas that others close to us believe feel like they don't fit for us, we often feel guilty, afraid, and even ashamed, like there's something wrong with us or bad about us.

So what do you trust? Do you trust other people's ideas and beliefs and your conditioning, or do you trust that little voice inside you that tells you something else? There seem to be two selves here: the conditioned self (the ego) that believes in following ideas and conditioning and another Self that feels differently.

Isn't it funny how everyone knows what the "little voice inside" is? We're born with an awareness of something other than our thoughts that is at times in conflict with our thoughts or other people's ideas. Even though this voice may go against our conditioning, we're often encouraged when we're young to pay attention to this voice. And if we didn't learn to do this as a child or we don't pay attention to this voice, we rather quickly learn that this voice does have something valuable to say! It can even save our life.

What is this voice? Well, it's not actually a voice but a knowing, a nudging, sometimes an uncomfortable feeling when we go against it. It is our intuition, our Heart, the "still, small voice within." We all know it, but we don't always listen to it because there's often a lot of pressure from others and even from ourselves in the form of fear and guilt to follow our conditioning and other people's ideas instead. However, people usually end up quite unhappy when they let their conditioning and other people's ideas determine their choices.

Unhappiness is not a good sign, although it's a common state. Unhappiness is usually a sign that we're not aligned with our personal truth—with what's true for us. We're not listening to our Heart. Understanding why we're unhappy is complicated by the fact that the ego is often unhappy and discontent even in the best of circumstances and possibly even when we *are* aligned with our plan. The ego complains about anything and everything. It is an ongoing voice of discontentment—the grass is always greener somewhere else. If we pay a lot of attention to the voice in our head, we're bound to be unhappy much of the time. So there is the usual unhappiness that's characteristic of the egoic state of consciousness, and there's the unhappiness that is a sign we aren't listening to our Heart or that we're out of step with our higher plan.

The unhappiness that indicates we aren't aligned with our plan is a deeper variety, a sense of our soul longing for something else, something more meaningful or more in tune with who we really are. This deeper unhappiness is often experienced as depression and often indicates that our life structures don't fit our plan. The cure generally calls for making different choices and possibly creating different life structures: changing our job or career, changing our relationship, moving, including something new in our life, developing an overlooked or a buried talent, or making some other important but possibly difficult change. This deeper unhappiness or depression is the "stick" that is attempting to get our attention and move us in another direction.

Joy is the "carrot" that says, "Go this way!" What a beautiful setup it is that joy is the sign that something is part of our higher plan! Do you want to know what your plan is? What do you love? Where is your joy, your juice, your excitement right now? The things that give you joy *right now* are part of your plan right now, not something that gave you joy in the past or something you think will give you joy in the future, but what gives you joy *right now*? All we can ever really know of our plan is what is true right now.

The fact that following our joy and doing what we love brings happiness and fulfillment is evidence that love and goodness are behind life. When joy and love are motivating us, the result is happiness, love, and goodness, not just for us as individuals, but for the Whole. Joy and love align us with our higher plan and with the Whole, and that can only be good for everyone.

Think about it: Has following your joy ever led to evil or harming someone? It just doesn't. Other people might not approve of what you love to do, but you aren't harming them by doing that, even if that's what they believe. On the other hand, negative emotions, especially fear, lead to all sorts of addictions and harm. But love is the opposite. Following love and joy leads to happiness and more love and joy, not just for you but ultimately for others too. If what you're doing is in your highest good, then it must be in everyone's highest good—in the highest good of the Whole.

What a great formula for life this is! Life is prodding us to follow our joy and love by rewarding us when we do that. This is very kind of Life. In providing us with this guidance system,

Life is being very loving. You could conclude that Life loves love and joy. You could conclude that love and joy are behind life. This Intelligence that has a plan loves and celebrates love! What's not to trust about that?

EVIL IS THE ABSENCE OF LOVE

If evil were behind life, this would be a sad world, indeed. As bad as it can get here, there are probably few people that feel that evil is what is behind this world. Certainly few want evil to be behind this world, and that's a good sign. Something in us wants and gravitates toward goodness, not evil. Negativity tugs at us and even grabs hold of us at times, but something else continually pulls us toward the opposite, toward love.

Just as darkness is the absence of light, evil is the absence of love. Evil isn't a reality itself but the result of the absence of contact with Reality, with what is true—love. Evil is the result of being divorced from our true nature, being very, very divorced, so divorced that someone might not even believe in love because he or she has so much fear and so much difficulty feeling love. Such deep separation is a frightening and lost place.

The spectrum of life is a spectrum of love: On one end is pure love and the experience of oneness with all life, and on the other end is the absence of love and the experience of complete separation and fear. What exists in the absence of love is fear, and fear can produce hateful acts.

Those who are lost in the deepest separation need our love and compassion; and yet, they are the ones who are most difficult to love. Nevertheless, no one is ever irretrievable. All eventually return to love. This journey on earth, which takes many, many lifetimes, is a return to love and a rediscovery of our oneness with all, in fact, of our true nature *as* Oneness. The journey is a beautiful one because it ends in love. It takes us away from separation and returns us to unity. This is surely evidence that love is behind all Life. We evolve from feeling very separate to realizing our oneness with all life. What a wonderful discovery and ending to this adventure called life. Life is good.

How do I know this? You don't have to take my word for it. Many, many have gone before us, and this is what they report and have reported. These individuals are the ones we revere as saints, spiritual masters, avatars, and founders of our religions. We revere them because we want the peace, love, and wisdom that they embody.

We want peace, love, and wisdom because these are what bring meaning and joy to life. Why? Because peace, love, and wisdom are what is behind life. We don't revere murderers and rapists or those who torture, maim, and steal from others. Why? Because we know what's true and good when we see it. We just know it. All societies value love. Love not only helps us survive by making it possible to cooperate with others, but love feels good; it just feels right. We know the rightness of love, and that is why we can trust life. Life is all about love.

LIFE PROVIDES

The ego focuses on what it wants that it doesn't have and on what's missing. It sees the glass as half empty. The ego was programmed to be this way, and it serves some purpose for survival. But the ego misses the truth: Life provides. Life doesn't provide everything the ego wants, but it provides what we need to fulfill our higher plan. Life is not about getting what the ego wants, although the ego would like it to be, but about learning, growing, and returning Home to love. For what life was designed to do, it is very dependable and trustworthy.

It's a good thing we can't trust life to give all of our egos what they want. What kind of a world would that be! Everyone would be rich, beautiful, young, and powerful and have everything they wanted. Perhaps the Creator made a world like that somewhere, but this isn't it! So we have to accept that. And, truly, that wouldn't be an ideal world, would it?

It would be wonderful if everyone were fed, clothed, and housed comfortably, and this would be more possible in a world that wasn't so ego-driven, in a world where we regarded others as equally valuable expressions of our own true Self. The ego has created a world with a lot of inequality, human rights abuses, environmental degradation, violence, and war, so let's not blame life for the damage and harm the ego has done and continues to do. Life on earth could and would be more wonderful for everyone with Essence at the helm instead of so many egos.

If we change any beliefs we have about life not providing to the belief that life provides exactly what we need, then we can begin to realize how very true this second statement is. We can begin to notice how beautifully life does provide what we need, and often even what we want. If, on the other hand, we believe that life doesn't provide well, then life will seem that way. That belief, like most beliefs, creates a particular internal experience of life, specifically, an experience of lack and discontentment, which affects how we are in life and what we do and consequently how we experience life and what we create in life.

If you want to change how you experience life, then you have to change what you believe about life. If you believe that life provides what you need, which happens to be true, then that's what you will experience. You will give life a chance to show you how it does do that, and you'll notice the ways that life already does do that. Then gratitude and joy will be alive within you, and they will fuel the creation of the life you want. With no negative beliefs to stop you, there is nothing left to do but follow your Heart and create the life you were meant to live.

Life provides in small ways and in big ways. It's important to notice the small ways because they aren't as insignificant as we might think. Many of the gifts life offers may not even be recognized initially. For example, I recently had tendonitis in my arms from too much computer work. A friend of mine that knew this had just discovered something that reduces inflammation because it had worked on her knee, so she excitedly told me about it. I dismissed her suggestion, thinking

I'd be fine if I just rested a few days. After a few weeks, I realized how serious my condition was and began taking the remedy and immediately improved. And here I am writing again.

Life provides. I'm sure you can come up with examples from your own experience of help arriving just when you needed it through information on the internet, a book, a friend, someone just showing up, or some other means. The Whole takes care of itself this way. Apparently, the Whole was agreeable to me returning to the computer. If it hadn't been, I may not have found a solution when I did.

Here's another example. Yesterday, a young couple came over to our house to express their gratitude to my husband for telling them about a healer named Braco, because the woman's sight had been corrected after traveling to Las Vegas to see this healer. That was a wonderful enough example of life providing, but they had another interesting story to tell about this trip.

They were staying at a campground in Las Vegas because they didn't have any money, but it was extremely hot there. They happened to meet a man from India at the campground who, after noticing how hot they were, said: "I accidently got a room at a hotel with two king size beds, and you're welcome to stay with me." Although they were a little wary of this offer, they decided to accept it. Then, the man handed them a one-hundred dollar bill and told them to go shopping for food and bring it to the hotel. In the hotel room, they had a wonderful feast, which the couple was very grateful for, since they hadn't eaten for a while. At bedtime, the man laid his wallet, keys, and cell phone on a table and said, "Take anything you need. I'm going to sleep." Of course they didn't take anything, but that's how trusting this man was!

This gentleman graciously provided the couple with exactly what they needed, without them even asking for anything. This is Essence in action. What a gift! And this story of how life provides was just what I needed today for this chapter!

Over a period of twenty years when I had very little money, but always enough, I discovered for myself life's generosity and trustworthiness. I would be down to my last dollar, and then money would show up, sometimes through others—inheritance, gifts, offers of support, forgotten savings accounts—but also through clients and other opportunities to make money.

In my thirties and forties, I lived a lifestyle that was not unlike that of a nun in its simplicity, solitude, and focus on contemplation. That lifestyle served me well, although it wasn't the lifestyle I'd expected. The things many people had in their lives at that age—a family, a house, and a career in the world— didn't seem to be in the cards for me.

Sometimes I felt shame over not having the usual things, but most of the time I felt great peace and gratitude for the simplicity of my life compared to those striving to achieve the American dream. I've never been part of the rat race. I've rarely been anything but self-employed and then not very employed. This afforded me more freedom and time than most people, enabling me to do the studying, meditation, writing, and inner work that formed the foundation for what I do now.

During those years, I loved how I spent my days; however, reconciling the lifestyle I was living with the one most people live wasn't that easy. Was it okay for me to do all the things I loved and not work in the world? Would I be okay? Would I survive? What will happen to me in the future? When I tried working in the world, it never worked out or felt right. Was there something wrong with me? I wondered. But mostly, I was just happy to have the opportunity to spend my days doing what I felt moved to do.

Somehow I managed financially. It almost seems like a miracle now—how I lived on so little. Maybe it was. It was the miracle of life supporting me doing what I loved doing and, apparently, what I was meant to do, even though at the time I wasn't that sure I was meant to do those things. Who is meant to spend their days meditating, studying, writing, and doing inner work? And yet, life supported me in doing these things.

There weren't many models in America for the lifestyle I was living, nor much appreciation for it. So I had doubts, and other people in my life had doubts—which was difficult. But in the end, my Heart and the opportunities life presented me with—or didn't present me with—created a life that nourished and supported my spirit and higher purpose. And I learned to be happy with little.

This is a good place to put a plug in for financial limitation. Most of us are very afraid of not having enough money, and many are willing to do almost anything to have what they feel is enough money. What is enough money?

When you have very little, you often discover how little you need compared to what you thought you needed. Financial limitation is an opportunity to discover the beauty of living simply and how to be happy with less. When you don't have the usual things that make the ego happy, you have to find a way to be happy without those things.

Financial limitation taught me so much. I am more fearless now—I'm not afraid of having little or afraid I won't have enough. I'm grateful for everything I have, and I enjoy the little things in life. I don't need money to be happy. That's freedom. And when you don't need money to be happy, it's easy to be generous when you do have something to share. When you trust life to provide, giving is easy. Money comes and goes as needed.

I would have to agree that it's no fun not having enough money to pay for the basics of life, and I'm not singing the praises of that, although I discovered that even when I thought I wouldn't have enough for the basics, I did. I'm really speaking to those of you who have what you need and still worry about not having enough. Worrying is the worst part of having little, and it doesn't change our situation or even motivate us in a way that's helpful.

Fear and worry do often motivate us but usually in the direction the ego suggests. How might Essence move you instead? You won't find out if you're wrapped up in your ego's fears and following your ego's solutions to those fears. The problem with worry and fear is that they keep us ego identified. It's the ego that is worried and afraid, and the ego is the only thing that is. Worry and fear don't come from Essence, and they keep us from Essence.

There's no reason for worry or fear because they don't serve us in any way. They don't keep us safe or warn us of anything real. Worry and fear are not connected to reality—to what is true *now*—but are produced by our imagination. The Being that we are naturally takes care of itself and knows how to do that. People who have difficulty taking care of themselves are usually not in touch sufficiently with their own inner wisdom, which has solutions to any situation. They're spinning around in their egoic mind, frantically trying to figure out what to do. Unfortunately, the egoic mind doesn't actually know what to do next and how to live life, although it pretends to. Listening to the egoic mind results in confusion and inappropriate or unnecessary actions.

The ego is confused and fearful, and that state isn't conducive to finding solutions. The ego's solution to being safe and secure is to move toward whatever will bring more power, money, recognition, status, and the like. The ego is what creates a sense of not being safe and secure and then it drives us toward what it thinks will help us relax and feel secure. But the ego's solutions don't work because the feelings of being unsafe and insecure come from the ego, not from our circumstances.

It's entirely possible to feel safe and secure with no money in our pocket. Feeling safe and secure is a state of mind, and it comes from dropping out of the egoic state of mind into Essence, not from getting more of anything the ego wants. The only reason we feel more secure when we finally get what the ego wants, such as more money, is because the ego relaxes for the time being, and the absence of fear drops us into Essence, which is a state of peace and trust in life, a state of feeling safe and secure. The good news is that, regardless of how little is in our bank account, we can be in Essence and in peace. However, the fear stirred up by having little money makes it challenging to experience the peace of our true nature.

Out of fear, the ego often takes us in directions we don't even need to go. This is only a problem when those directions are at odds with the direction Essence would take us. Then we miss out on something more fulfilling. We can follow the egoic mind or we can follow Essence. Following Essence is not only the choice that makes us happier, but also the safer choice because Essence's solutions are wise. Essence is on our side. It's in the business of supporting us in life, and it is capable of doing that.

Many fear that following their Heart will mean living in poverty, and sometimes people do make less money doing what makes their Heart sing. But many very successful people get there by following their Heart. Many of the people we admire for their accomplishments didn't let other people's opinions and ideas interfere with doing what felt important and meaningful to them, no matter how little money it might mean. Many successful people are risk-takers, meaning they risked following a path others might not have taken out of fear.

The truth is, we don't really know if following our Heart will mean living on less money. The ego and other people's egos generally believe it will, but that isn't necessarily true. In any event, when we're doing what makes our Heart sing, material things and the other superficial things the ego cares about don't matter that much because we're happy doing what we're doing. We don't need those things to be happy. They're put in proper perspective.

However, when we're unhappy, because we aren't doing what we love, we turn to the things the ego finds comfort in to try to feel good and get happy: We eat, shop, take drugs, drink, become a workaholic, or act out some other form of addiction. Unfortunately, indulging too much in these things only makes us feel bad about ourselves and even more unhappy and strengthens the ego's hold on us. We become out of balance and out of touch with our true nature. And so we suffer.

HOW LIFE PROVIDES

Life provides in many ways, not just by others giving us money, information, help, and other things we need, although that happens all the time. One of the most obvious ways Life provides is by presenting us with opportunities that further our growth and life purpose. We may or may not take advantage of those opportunities, in which case, life will present us with other ones. Life never stops attempting to lead us to where it wants us to go, to what will evolve us, support us, fulfill us, and make us happy.

Less obviously, Life also provides by giving us the body, intelligence, talents, personality, drives, intuition, and ability to say and do what we need to do to fulfill our higher plan. We have a unique role to play in the Whole, and it requires us to be uniquely the way we are. We aren't supposed to be like anyone else, but exactly the way we are.

Most basically, life provides us with a body and mind to live this life as we were meant to. We look exactly as we are meant to look, and we are as smart as we are meant to be too. Life also provides us with just the right personality for our life's lessons and goals. Some personality traits present challenges for us and some make life easier. The personality we have is no mistake, just as our physical appearance and intelligence are no mistake. Our personality traits are encoded in our genes and are meant to bring us certain experiences and lessons, develop certain kinds of talents, and help us accomplish our life purpose. For example, if our life purpose needs courage, initiative, and leadership, we will be encoded with those traits.

Astrology is the study of the personality and psychological drives and the challenges associated with that personality and those drives. Astrology gives us a glimpse into the intentions of the Whole and what we came into life to accomplish and learn. Nothing else offers as much information about ourselves as psychological and spiritual beings as astrology does. For more than twenty years, astrology was invaluable to me in counseling others about their spiritual lessons and life purpose. I no longer work with individuals, but I recommend getting to know your chart by talking with one of the many highly skilled astrologers that are available these days.

As difficult as it may be to believe that astrology could possibly be valid, enough experience with astrology will convince anyone that it is valid. Astrology works and it's helpful. Those who believe that astrology isn't valid haven't investigated it fully; those who believe it's valid know from living with it.

We choose our personality specifically for how it can serve our lessons and life purpose. When I say we choose our personality, I mean that before being born, our soul makes some decisions about what it intends to learn and accomplish in the coming lifetime, and it chooses circumstances, such as a family an environment, and a personality, accordingly. If this isn't part of your belief system, please bear with me while I present a few metaphysical ideas because they're crucial in explaining why life is trustworthy.

If you don't believe we live other lifetimes, it's likely to be difficult to reconcile the inequalities of birth, that is, why someone is born with easier circumstances, greater abilities, or more wisdom than another. If you believe we live just one lifetime, it's quite difficult to believe that Life is just and trustworthy in the face of these inequalities. One of the reasons I accepted reincarnation into my belief system is that it helped me be more compassionate and understanding of the differences between people and to feel that life was meaningful and good.

Our beliefs are important, and if your beliefs aren't helping you be more loving, compassionate, and trusting of life, then maybe those beliefs need to be questioned. We never know for sure what is true about life, so why not choose whatever takes you toward love and compassion and away from fear and other negativity?

Beliefs that don't serve love aren't worth holding, no matter who says they're true. In the end, the buck stops with you. You are the one living your life and accountable for the consequences of your beliefs. If what you believe isn't leading to happiness, peace, love, compassion, and goodness, then why keep believing those things? If God is love, and most religions claim this, then it seems safe to discard beliefs that don't lead to love and to adopt ones that do. If you do that, you'll be discarding a lot of beliefs and adopting a few very simple ones! But you won't miss those discarded beliefs.

Life also provides us with the inner guidance we need to learn our lessons. Whenever we face a challenge—something we can grow from—our inner wisdom encourages us to take the high road, see what we need to see, and learn what we need to learn. It encourages us to respond and react with love, acceptance, gratitude, patience, and wisdom to whatever we're going through.

We all have the potential to act with integrity in any situation, and in most situations, we innately know what that would look like, although we don't necessarily act that way. Our inner wisdom urges us not to indulge in the ego's automatic reactions, self-pity, anger, blame, hatred, jealousy, resentment, judgment, or unkindness. It speaks to us softly, intuitively, and doesn't push like the ego's voice. Our inner wisdom is so allowing that it even allows us to make a bad choice. Life is benevolent enough to show us when we've made a bad choice by providing us with a bad result, including suffering. Bad choices lead to bad results. How kind of Life to teach us this way. We can trust its guidance.

Our inner wisdom also guides us toward fulfilling our higher plan. It urges us: "Go this way!" "Don't go that way!" If we don't listen, this voice is benevolent enough to allow us this choice, while continuing to try to move us in certain directions and not others. It gives us constant feedback about how we're doing and what to do next by urging us toward our joy and away from what causes suffering.

THE LAW OF KARMA

Just as there are physical laws that govern the physical world, there are spiritual laws that govern us, as conscious co-creators of life. Like our physical laws, these spiritual laws are trustworthy because they are consistent and work reliably, although we might not be aware of their workings. They are also trustworthy because they teach love and take us Home to our true nature.

One of these laws is the law of karma. Karma is the Great Teacher. It teaches us what we need to learn. Life is a school, and we're here to have experiences and learn from them. Above all, we're here to learn to love. Karma teaches by virtue of our actions causing a reaction: We do something, and we get a response from life or from someone, although that response might not be immediate. That response provides feedback about our actions, and that feedback is the teaching.

A simple example of this is when we are kind, others are generally kind in return, and so our kindness is rewarded and reinforced. Even if others aren't kind in return (because they're free to choose to not be kind), being kind is its own reward. Being unkind works the same way: When we're unkind, others generally respond unkindly, and our unkindness is not rewarded or reinforced. And, regardless of how others respond, being unkind doesn't feel good (except maybe briefly to the ego), so behaving this way isn't reinforced internally.

Whatever we put out in the world, tends to come back to us, although not necessarily right away. Whether feedback from others or from life about our actions is immediate or not, we receive feedback instantly internally: When we act in accordance with our true nature—with love—we feel good; when we don't, we don't feel good. This is how life teaches us love: It rewards us for love and doesn't reward the opposite. So if life is rewarding loving behavior, what does that mean? This would seem to be evidence for a loving force behind life, a force that is guiding us toward love and away from whatever undermines love.

It's easiest to see karma at work in our relationships because the feedback is often so immediate and obvious. But karma also delivers our major life lessons, and in those cases, the workings of karma are not so obvious. We might experience some difficulty or limitation and not realize that it's a karmic lesson. If we've done something that goes against life, then sometime in this lifetime or another, we'll meet with an experience designed to teach us whatever we need to learn so that we don't continue that behavior.

Some karma, by necessity, teaches by withholding something pleasant or delivering something unpleasant. However, a lot of karma teaches in ways that don't appear punitive at all. When life can teach something without presenting us with something difficult, it will. The purpose of karma is to teach, not to punish.

For instance, if someone abuses another, the abuser needs to learn love (most abusers were unloved as children). This isn't taught by experiencing abuse, but by experiencing the opposite—love. The abuser might be required to atone to the victim in some other lifetime through good works or other benefits, but the lesson the abuser needs would not be delivered by being abused.

No one deserves abuse, and abuse serves no purpose and is damaging in ways that can take lifetimes to heal. Abuse happens because people have egos, and egos sometimes abuse others. Often victims do develop more compassion as a result of abuse, but that's no excuse for abuse. Compassion can be learned in other ways than by being abused. Nevertheless, sometimes an older soul will put himself or herself in harm's way because it serves that soul's life purpose to experience abuse. For example, someone whose life purpose is to help battered women might choose to experience this. But this is very different from someone experiencing abuse when it isn't part of his or her soul's plan.

Some would argue that "bad guys" get away with a lot in life—so where's the karma, then? What goes around doesn't necessarily come around *immediately*. Some karmic lessons can't be taught until another lifetime because circumstances don't allow it. The soul designs lessons carefully, and a lesson might require that the person be born into a particular circumstance or another country or be a different gender or race or have a very different appearance or personality.

Reincarnation and karma offer an explanation for many of the inequities in life that, without such an explanation, might result in our concluding that life is random, uncaring, and unfair, which isn't true. Within the scope of our entire span of lifetimes, each soul experiences every extreme and nearly every possible experience. What isn't often appreciated is that our soul chooses to have even the difficult experiences. It embraces the opportunity for growth that such experiences provide.

Many of our challenges are the normal challenges of a soul as it evolves here on earth, while others are the result of karma and the need to learn a particular lesson. Through these challenges, we learn to navigate the worst of circumstances. We learn that our attitude and beliefs are critical to how much we suffer during these experiences, which is one of the most important lessons we can learn in life. Even under very extreme circumstances, it's possible to suffer very little, and that is evidence of the goodness of life.

Having beliefs that help explain life's inequities, inequalities, and challenges is very important. If your beliefs about life and God leave you feeling angry, depressed, afraid, empty, or hopeless, then trusting life and opening to the experience of Essence will be more difficult. Beliefs that keep you angry at or afraid of life tie you to the ego, and that's a place of suffering and limitation.

Love and goodness are behind life, and if that isn't how you see life, you won't experience the happiness, peace, and joy that are always available. It's important to examine our beliefs and weed out the ones that don't work for us. As children, we don't have the resources for doing this, so it falls upon us as adults to do this work. It may seem difficult to change your beliefs, but it isn't as difficult as you might think. I will give you some tools for doing this in the last chapter.

Over our many lifetimes, our mistakes and transgressions are corrected and balanced and we learn to embody our true nature more fully. Our experiences hone and shape us, and we become kinder, more loving human beings, not the opposite. Although some people might backslide and seem to devolve and become more selfish and less loving, over our many lifetimes, we all eventually become wonderful human beings. Evolution moves us toward love.

This can be deduced from the presence of individuals who are already very loving. How did they get this way? Were they born that way? Some people are born more loving; this isn't just a matter of upbringing and environment. Any parent who has had a number of children can attest to how different each is. Even children in the same family can differ greatly in what you could call their spiritual evolution—their wisdom and ability to love.

We learn to love over our many lifetimes, so those who've lived more lifetimes have a greater capacity to love than others, a greater capacity to not be identified with the ego. Some people are also wiser than others, which relates both to a lack of ego identification and to lessons learned in earlier lifetimes. We are in different grades in this school called life, but we all eventually graduate; we all return to the Oneness from which we came.

Over our many lifetimes, we learn to embody the qualities of our true nature: love, patience, empathy, compassion, acceptance, tolerance, peacefulness, forgiveness, wisdom, gratitude, and trust in life. Most would agree that these are admirable and desirable qualities, even if we don't entirely embody them ourselves. Why is that? Wouldn't this be evidence for love being at our core? And if that's so, wouldn't love be at the core of life as well? And given that, couldn't you conclude that life is trustworthy?

I'm appealing to your rational side here for a reason. The reason we distrust life is not rational. The ego isn't rational. It just distrusts life. That's just how it feels about life, and all the more so if anything happened in our childhood that undermined our trust. If we don't question the ego's distrust, that distrust remains with us. This argument for trusting life is meant to counteract the ego's irrational position of distrust, which seems to be our default position as human beings. If we don't examine our programming, then we will be at the mercy of it. Programming, after all, is programming and very often unconscious. If we make our programming conscious and examine it objectively, we stand a chance of moving beyond any programming that is untrue and limiting.

The ego doesn't see life as it is, but as the ego is programmed to see life. The ego is our software, and our software doesn't give us an accurate picture of reality nor does it accept reality the way it is. So that's what we are up against in learning to trust reality and see the truth about it: Life is good.

ASK AND YOU SHALL RECEIVE

Another spiritual law that is evidence for life being good and supportive is: "Ask and you shall receive." People sometimes bemoan the fact that they don't get what they pray for. They may assume this is evidence of an uncaring or perhaps nonexistent God. Not getting what they want is a big reason why many don't trust God or life, as if there is no wisdom in Life not always delivering what we want.

There's a caveat to "Ask and you shall receive" and that is "if it is in your highest good and the good of the Whole." Do you really want something if it isn't in your highest good and the good of the Whole? Not really. "Ask and you shall receive" means you will get what you ask for if it's best for all concerned. We don't understand the workings or needs of the Whole, so we aren't in a position to judge what is best, although our ego assumes it knows. This is a self-centered and short-sighted assumption on the part of the ego.

Are you willing to have *Thy* will be done, not just *my* will? When we pray for Thy will to be done, it is always done. The only thing that can interfere with Thy will being done is our own free will. When we pray for something that is contrary to Thy will, sometimes we do get it if it serves our growth to have it, so then that lesson becomes Thy will. As they say, "Be careful what you wish for!" But often, when we pray for something the ego wants, we don't get it because getting it would interfere with Thy will, or our higher plan.

The problem is not only that we may be asking for the wrong thing when we pray, but that we may not ask at all for something that would benefit us, something that Life wants for us. We were given free will, and spiritual forces that guide the unfolding of our life plan are very careful not to infringe on our free will. Asking shows a readiness and willingness on our part to receive whatever we're asking for, so spiritual forces wait for us to ask before giving us certain things.

An example of something Life might want for us and be willing to give us but that we may be blocking consciously or unconsciously is emotional healing. If we deny our need for emotional healing or if we're unwilling to take steps to heal, then spiritual forces will wait until we're ready. On the other hand, if we ask for help to move beyond our emotional pain or limiting beliefs, we'll receive it. It might come in the form of a book, teacher, or healer coming into our life or a flow of insights that free us from stuck and limited ways of thinking. Life brings us what we need when we're ready for it. We show that we're ready for it by asking for it.

Life wants certain things for all of us and is willing to bring them to us: healing, growth, evolution, love, peace, wisdom, fulfilling activities, creativity, fun, discovery, and pleasure. Life loves all these things, and the Being that we are is here to experience all of them. When we ask for these things, they will come into our life some way. On the other hand, if we ask for something the ego wants—to win the lottery, a particular person to fall in love with us, a dream house, an expensive car—we may or may not get it. And if we do get it, having it might turn out to be more of a lesson than the experience we hoped it would be. Then again, sometimes Essence wants for us exactly what our ego wants.

Everyone has spiritual forces—spirit guides or angels—connected to them that assist their growth, healing, and evolution. Opening to them and requesting their aid is an excellent prayer. These forces are always assisting us in their usual ways, but they can help us more fully when we invite them to. Asking for their help is a powerful act because our requests are always answered as long as they fit with our higher plan. Believing spiritual forces exist to help us is important because if we don't, we won't call on them and they won't be able to help us to the extent that they can.

Our actions do speak louder than words, so prayers without a true intention won't necessarily be heard, while a strong intention, even without words, will be. For instance, if we say we want healing but we continue to enjoy our negative thoughts, then our allegiance is clearly to those thoughts. On the other hand, if we're making an effort to meditate and do things to clear negativity, then spiritual forces rejoice in that intention and help us do that.

Our intentions are clear to spiritual forces. They respect our choice to wallow in negativity if we choose to do that, but they are poised to help us as soon as we ask for help or begin taking steps to free ourselves from negativity. Going to spiritual retreats, meditating, reading spiritual books, going to healers, praying, and in other ways steeping ourselves in the positive and in environments that are healing sends a powerful message that we are ready and willing to receive the help, healing, and insights we need to be happier and more at peace. If trusting life is an issue for you, declare that you are ready to see that life

is trustworthy now, and invite the spiritual forces that work
with you to help you with this.

LOVE IS WHAT DRIVES LIFE

Coming through vision, coming through wisdom,
Coming together–this love!
Giving me daytime, giving this nighttime,
Bringing within me this love!

From the song "Change We Must"
from *Change We Must* by Jon Anderson

Fear drives the ego, but love drives life. Love drives all that
matters in life. Love is the motivating force in life that creates,
sustains, enhances, and gives meaning to life. There is nothing
else here but love because Life *is* love. We *are* love.

This Love is hidden only by a *sense* of being someone who
is afraid of life. Our identity as a separate individual is of
someone who feels lacking, insignificant, lost, confused, afraid,
struggling, and in conflict with life. So it's no wonder the ego
wants and feels it needs so much to be okay and happy. But
this is a false identity and false needs—we need nothing but
what we already have to be happy.

We are not the individual we *think* we are. We *are* life. It is
living through us. And when the ego is put aside, Life lives
through us more cleanly and purely, and with ease, gratitude,
fortitude, joy, and love. When the ego is no longer dominant,
it becomes obvious that all that's here is Essence *being* and
relishing in being.

Life is trustworthy because love is behind life. Love is what is unfolding life and making life happen. Love is the motivating force in all we do: Love for our life, our body, and food motivates us to grow, shop for, prepare, and eat what we need to sustain us. Love for self-expression, expansion, discovery, and self-development motivates us to speak, learn, create, expand our capabilities, and develop our talents. Love for others motivates us to procreate, relate, give, care for, nurture, and support others and society. Love for pleasure and fun motivates us to play, rest, sing, dance, and enjoy life. Love for security and safety motivates us to be careful and take care of ourselves. Love for being productive motivates us to work and develop our skills. Love for knowledge motivates us to learn, read, and share what we've learned.

Love allows us to identify with the ego, and love is even what motivates the ego: Love for security, safety, self-preservation, superiority, power, comfort, and prestige motivate the ego to pursue what it pursues, such as money, beauty, and a good job.

The ego and Essence are motivated to do many of the same things: Both motivate us to take care of ourselves, work, play, pursue relationships, and in other ways create a life. However, the ego and Essence do these things for different reasons. While Essence does them for the love of life, the love of being alive, and the drive to perpetuate life, the ego does them out of feelings of lack and fear in order to gain superiority and control. Because the ego acts from fear, it often causes harm, but even love is behind that, albeit a distorted version of it: love for what the ego is trying to get by harming someone or love for its own self-preservation.

Because the ego sees itself as separate from everything, it is driven by fear and sees others and the world as something to conquer or subdue. This is obvious in how people have related to the environment. While native peoples have generally viewed themselves as part of a Whole and as belonging to and caretakers of nature, our ego-driven societies have related to the environment and other peoples as something to control and use for our own needs, without considering the impact of our actions on the Whole. These are two very different ways of being, which come from very different states of consciousness and result in very different worlds. If we don't begin to relate to the world more from Essence instead of the ego, there may not be much of a world left. Raising our consciousness is not just for ourselves, but for everyone and for the earth—for the Whole.

Many think that if they don't live as the ego would have them live, they'll end up doing nothing. They think that spiritual teachings that emphasize meditation, acceptance, and being in the moment lead to being passive and avoiding the world and practical matters. Many assume they won't get anything done or be able to pay their bills if they live as these teachings suggest. But that's a misunderstanding. These teachings emphasize what they do because doing these things drops us into Essence, where we can then discover how Essence is moving us to act *now* in the world and what wisdom and insights it might have for us that can inform our life and actions. How do we know what to do and how to live our life?

Instead of getting the answers from the egoic mind, we can find out by paying attention to what's coming out of the Now.

Life happens, and it happens through us. We can be moved by the ego and its fear, or we can let life happen through us as it's meant to by letting Essence move us. Essence is motivated by love, not by fear, and the results of Essence moving through us are peace, harmony, unity, and love. The only thing that can interfere with wiser and more loving action in this world is following the ego's fear and letting the ego dominate our lives. When we're no longer listening to the egoic mind, Life has a chance to flow through us as it's meant to and as it naturally does, even to some extent when we are ego identified.

Everyone knows what it's like to live from Essence: Life is happening, and you are flowing with it. Sometimes you are the actor, and sometimes you are responding to whatever's happening. When we're living from Essence, we move naturally and spontaneously through life, accomplishing what we need to accomplish and enjoying life every step of the way. When we're in Essence, our actions are more functional and effective than when we're ego identified because they are what's called for in the moment—no more no less—and because our experience of life isn't cluttered by unnecessary thoughts or troubled by unnecessary feelings, which drain our energy. Life is much simpler and happier when we're in touch with who we really are than when we're believing we are alone and separate and that life is a struggle. The ego makes life a struggle, but life doesn't have to be that way.

In summary, we can trust life because:

- *Life is consistently the way it is—we can trust it to be the way it is.*

- *The fact that we can't predict what will happen next in our life isn't a sign of life being untrustworthy, but an indication of a higher plan at work. For the Divine to have the experience it intends as a human being and to have the experience of free will, it's necessary for humans to not know what's going to happen; it's necessary for life to be unpredictable.*

- *Joy and love are what guide life. When we go toward what we love and what brings us joy, we are rewarded with happiness. When we don't, we feel unhappy. Life is very loving in providing us with this guidance system. We can conclude from this that love is behind life and that therefore life is trustworthy.*

- *Evil is the absence of love. Goodness and love are at the core of life, not evil.*

- *Life provides us with the programming and inner and outer resources we need to learn what we came into life to learn and fulfill our life purpose.*

- *Just as there are physical laws that make life consistent and therefore trustworthy, there are spiritual laws that make life trustworthy. These laws teach us love, not the opposite, and they are designed to take us Home.*

- *Life brings us what we need when we are ready for it. We show that we are ready for it by asking for it.*

- *Love drives all that we do. Love is the motivating force in life that creates, sustains, enhances, and gives meaning to life. There's nothing else here but love because Life is love. We are love. This Love is hidden only by a sense of being someone who is afraid of life.*

* * *

Since love is lord of heaven and earth,
How can I keep from singing?

From the song "How Can I Keep from Singing?"
from *Shepherd Moons* by Enya

CHAPTER 4
What Guides Your Life?

WHAT DO YOU BELIEVE ABOUT GOD?

The answer to the question, "What guides life?" can only be intuited, not really known in the way we know some fact. You'll never know if the answer you come up with to this question is absolutely true. However, not knowing something doesn't necessarily stop us from believing something, from forming beliefs about it, either consciously or unconsciously. So another question is: "What do you *believe* guides life?" Also, "Do you believe anything guides life?"

Your beliefs matter; they affect how you experience life and what you do or don't do. So first of all, do you believe something is guiding life? And if so, is it benevolent or not? If you believe nothing is guiding life, what effect does that belief have on you? And what do you believe in place of that? What do you believe about life, and how does that affect you? This is a very important question. And when I say "believe," I don't just mean intellectually, but what do you *really* believe, deep down, in your bones, because those are the beliefs that underlie your feelings and actions.

Our beliefs are part of our programming. Unless we examine them, they have effects we may not be aware of. That's fine if the effects are good—if your beliefs lead to peace, happiness, love, fulfillment, and exuberance for life—but not so good if they lead to confusion, sadness, anger, depression, hopelessness, selfishness, not caring about others, or not wanting to participate in life. Some people have programming, or conditioning, that dooms them to unhappiness for as long as that programming is unconscious, while others have programming that allows them to be in Essence and be led by Essence to fulfill their life purpose. The good news is that our programming can be changed, and this is accomplished most effectively by first becoming aware of what we believe.

Can we agree that a belief is worthwhile if it leads to happiness, fulfillment, and more love and peace for ourselves and others? And can we agree that a belief is not as worthwhile if it leads to harming others, confusion, unhappiness, despair, anger, hostility, sadness, and other negative emotions? If we can't know whether a belief is actually true or not, like a belief in God or a belief in a guiding force, can we at least agree that beliefs that lead to love and other results we as humans consider beneficial and desirable are worthwhile, while beliefs that lead to the opposite results are not? I'm arguing here that the value and the truth of a belief is in what effect it has on us to believe it.

This way of viewing beliefs puts the responsibility on us for choosing what we believe. We have already chosen what we believe, but that choosing happened unconsciously for the most part. Whether we realize it or not, we are all living according to certain beliefs. We acquired many of them almost as if by osmosis, and that's very different from consciously choosing to believe them. For example, children who are abused don't consciously choose to believe they're inferior, but they still believe it, and they believe it on a very deep level. Our unconscious beliefs are some of the strongest beliefs we have.

Examining what we believe is important work because many of our beliefs are limiting. I could suggest you just throw all your beliefs out the window and be done with it, since we actually don't need our beliefs to live good lives, as radical as that may sound, but you'd only be able to throw out the beliefs you were conscious of. So to get beyond all our negative and limiting beliefs, we still have to make our unconscious beliefs conscious. Then, we can throw them out! This work isn't as hard as you might think because it mainly involves asking questions and listening quietly inside for answers. This kind of examination is often referred to as *inquiry*.

The purpose of this inquiry is to uncover and clear out our negative and limiting beliefs—the ones that don't serve, ones that lead to results we don't want and don't deserve. We can use the guideline of love to determine which beliefs serve us and serve life and which ones don't: Beliefs that lead to love serve us and serve life, and beliefs that don't lead to love neither serve us nor life. Using this guideline, do your beliefs about what is guiding life serve you and serve life? Do they serve love, that is, does holding those beliefs make you a more loving person and, consequently, more aligned with Essence?

The reason love works as a guideline is that love is our essential nature. If we're believing something that helps us experience love, then that belief resonates or is compatible with our true nature, with reality, with what's true about life. If, on the other hand, we're believing something that takes us away from love—away from the experience of our true nature— then we're believing something that isn't compatible with our true nature, with reality, with what's true about life. This is quite a simple guideline, and it works.

A simple question to ask yourself that can be useful and captures this guideline is: "Does this belief bring me into Essence or take me out of Essence?" By this I mean, does a belief bring you into a state of peace and love or out of this state, does it cause you to relax and feel at peace with life or stir up negative emotions?

The ego might come in at this point with the argument that we also have to survive, and all this talk about love isn't going to pay the bills! The ego would argue there are other values more important than love, more essential to survival. The ego would have us believe that its values and beliefs are more suited to survival. But are they?

We've survived as a species not because we have an ego, but more in spite of it. Human beings have survived and flourished because they learned to cooperate with each other and share resources and knowledge. The ego didn't and doesn't make this easy. Something else, not the ego, is behind the creation of our societies, and that is love.

It's easy to see how love benefits survival. In the most basic sense, love bonds parents and children together, creating families, which are the building blocks of society. Without love, we wouldn't marry, procreate, build homes, cities, and countries. Love drives all these activities. Love is the glue that binds couples, families, and societies.

Love is also the attractive force that draws to us the help, companionship, information, and other things we need to flourish. Love creates the good karma that keeps the good going out and coming back, which makes the world go around. Evidence of the importance of love to survival can be seen in the homeless population, most of whom lack the connections with others, for whatever reason, that sustain most of us. Those who aren't able to maintain relationships, perhaps because of mental illness or other problems, often fall through the cracks of society. A loving society rescues them from their plight.

To return to the original question, "What do you believe guides life, if anything?" This is like asking, "Do you believe in God, and what do you believe about God?" This is a very essential question. The answer helps define what you value, how you see and experience life, how you see yourself and others, and what you do.

How we see God is often similar to how we saw our parents, and certainly likely to be similar to what our parents taught us about God. If we were parented strictly or harshly, our parents may have believed in a strict God and the axiom "spare the rod, spoil the child." We probably learned from them that God is punitive, and we learned to be afraid of God–afraid of life–and also to some extent afraid of others and of our own impulses and drives. If we were parented with a lot of compassion, our parents probably believed in a compassionate God and taught us that God is loving. Their kind treatment of us made it possible for us to be loving and to expect others and life to regard us lovingly.

Many receive great comfort from their religious beliefs because those beliefs help them feel and connect with a positive presence in life—with Essence, with God. Their beliefs help them realize the Divine within them and around them, to realize there is more to life than the world brought to us by our senses. On the other hand, some religious beliefs connect us with and keep us connected to our ego. Those are beliefs that cause us to feel afraid, guilty, or ashamed. Often the same religion does both—gives a sense of connection with the Divine *and* makes us feel inferior, afraid, and ashamed.

Unfortunately, most religions don't encourage us to be discriminating and to believe only some tenets and not others. We're expected to believe everything and sometimes even coerced with fear to accept everything without question. We're told we'll be punished for not believing; we'll be thrown into hell. How can this be? How can a religion that preaches love also have at its helm a God that sends people to hell simply for not believing something? The love part, I get. The hell part, I don't get because it doesn't ring true in my Heart. It doesn't even make sense in my head.

Fear belongs to the ego. Fear has been used throughout time to manipulate and control people. It's behind all wars and acts of violence. I can't believe that God, or whatever is behind life, is violent, although I know people can be violent when they're very afraid that they won't survive or when they believe they aren't worthwhile or something else that makes them feel they have to lash out. God can't be afraid enough to have violent feelings or need violence to convince people of certain beliefs or control them. This is an image of God that is fashioned from the basest instincts of humankind. Love and violence are not compatible in me; how can they be compatible in God? How could God do things to human beings that I wouldn't dream of doing? How can I be more evolved than God?

I'm sure that many of you reading this have already come to these same conclusions yourself. If so, what conclusions or beliefs do you now have about life and God? For a while, after leaving the religion I was brought up in, I felt quite empty until I found some beliefs that felt truer to me, ones that helped me remain connected to the God in my Heart–Essence. As a child, I loved God so much, and I loved the sacredness I felt when I was in church. After discarding my religious beliefs, I longed for that connection again. When I found it again, it didn't require a religious setting or dogma. All it required was for me to experience the goodness in my own being and to appreciate it in others. From that recognition of the Divine within, only good can come, and no particular beliefs are required except ones that help you find that place within yourself and remain there.

I love God, and I know that God is this love I have for what I'm calling God. How do I know it? I just do. Does it make me happy to feel it? Yes. More importantly, I'm happy not just because I feel it, but because feeling it moves me in my life in ways that also feel good and rewarding and in ways that make others feel good too. What could be more trustworthy than this love? If we go in the direction of love, we will never be off course.

One of the things that makes us human is our capacity to make conscious choices. We are free to choose what we believe, say, and do. We revere this freedom, and such freedom develops and sustains strong societies. Freedom is a basic value. To deny the right of children to question and think freely is an abomination and a detriment to society. We need to be teaching our children to think for themselves *and* follow their Heart, not to follow a set of prescribed beliefs, ones that we may not even have questioned ourselves.

It's not only our right, but also our responsibility to question our beliefs because we're responsible for where those beliefs lead. If your beliefs aren't helping you have a happier, more loving, and more fulfilling life but are, instead, causing you to feel inferior and afraid, then will you live in fear or not? You get to choose. Question your beliefs, and you don't need to live in fear. What will be left to guide you when your beliefs are gone is your Heart.

Each of us knows the truth of how to be in our lives. We can trust that—we can trust our Heart. What we can't trust is other people to know what's true in general or true specifically for us. Unless someone is in touch with Essence, he or she won't know the truth but only know the ego's truth, and that isn't the truth. Fortunately, we have what we need inside ourselves to navigate life lovingly and wisely.

Here's a quote attributed to Buddha, which I "happened" to find on Facebook right after completing this section. I'd never run across it before. Life provides:

*Do not believe in anything simply because you have heard it.
Do not believe in anything simply because it is spoken and
rumored by many. Do not believe in anything simply because
it is found written in your religious books. Do not believe in
anything merely on the authority of your teachers and elders.
Do not believe in traditions because they have been handed
down for many generations. But after observation and
analysis, when you find that anything agrees with reason and
is conducive to the good and benefit of one and all, then
accept it and live up to it.*

THE EGO AS GUIDE

The problem with having beliefs that cause us to distrust life is
that fearful beliefs keep us stuck in the ego and oriented
toward the ego's guidance instead of Essence's. Then we end
up trusting life even less because following the ego's guidance
doesn't lead to a very satisfying life. Living solely according to
our beliefs and other conditioning results in a life the ego or
other people's egos think we should live, not the life we were
meant to live. Fortunately, it's a rare individual who isn't
guided at least some of the time by the Heart.

The ego bases its advice and guidance on conditioning.
The ego *makes up* advice based on our knowledge, what's
happened before, and conclusions we've come to from our
experience and other people's. There's some value in this
information, but information alone has no inherent wisdom.
Information when misapplied or applied at the wrong time
turns out to be bad advice. Moreover, much of the

information the ego draws from for its advice is inaccurate, contradictory, and outdated, and many of the conclusions are erroneous and therefore can't be counted on to be helpful.

Why do so many people make choices they later regret? Because they're listening to the counsel of their ego—they're listening to their thoughts or other people's thoughts, beliefs, and opinions. But how useful are those beliefs and opinions for knowing how to live your life in this moment? What's the guidance or advice that's right for you right *now?* This moment is absolutely unique, and it requires advice that fits you now, not advice that fit some other time or that might fit in the future or that fit someone else at some point.

Where does good advice come from? It can only come out of the moment if it is to be right for the moment. But the egoic mind is usually in the past or future. So that's the problem. The egoic mind isn't tuned into *now* but some other point in time. To know what's right for us right now, we have to pay attention to the Heart, which continually opens and closes in response to what's happening and delivers intuitions, wisdom, drives, inspiration, and insights that are perfectly fitted to us right now.

Simultaneously, as the Heart is delivering its guidance, the ego also produces guidance about what to do and say in the form of thoughts, desires, and feelings, and these are what end up guiding most people's lives. This is all well and good, as it produces the lessons and growth each of us is meant to experience. Our conditioning is our programming, and this programming isn't a mistake. We are meant to grow and evolve by responding to it. However, this growth can be quite painful, and at a certain point in our evolution, we discover we can move beyond this programming and live more in tune with our true nature, where we still grow and evolve but not so painfully.

There comes a point in everyone's spiritual evolution—in their evolution as a human being—to begin to live more from the Heart and less from the ego. You are undoubtedly at this point or you wouldn't be reading this and other similar teachings. So life is providing you with the understanding you need to move beyond the ego and its suffering toward greater happiness, peace, love, and fulfillment.

Thoughts are so much a part of us that it seems odd to consider that we don't actually need them and that they are, in fact, the problem, not the solution we thought they were. We're programmed to believe the wrong thing! We're programmed to believe our thoughts instead of our Heart. That creates the suffering and challenges that lead to the growth our soul intends—until it doesn't intend that particular kind of growth anymore.

Once we become more aware of our thoughts and take time to examine and question them, we discover just how untrue and untrustworthy they actually are. We're programmed to believe our thoughts are trustworthy! How funny. Just to be clear, our rational mind *is* trustworthy: We can trust it to analyze, deduce, evaluate, and understand. What we can't trust is the egoic mind, the very personal voice in our head that rattles on about anything and everything. It's the rational mind that's able to see the uselessness and falseness of the voice in our head. So we use the rational mind to see through the aspect of mind that seems to be our own very special thoughts. The rational mind, unlike the egoic mind, doesn't have a voice but is simply a tool we use to evaluate ideas, including our own thoughts.

Once we stop seeing this voice in our head as being our own voice and being a voice of wisdom and truth, the illusion is busted! Once we realize that it's a lie that this voice is wise and trustworthy, we can't ever view this voice the same way again. This is a huge step in our evolution, a great step toward freedom from the ego and the suffering it causes.

It's easy to be convinced by the voice in our head because it's meant to be convincing. But just because this voice seems true doesn't mean it is true! Con men can also be very convincing, and it's wise to not believe them. It's wise to not identify with the voice in our head, to realize it doesn't reflect who we are but only our programming.

If you're able to see this voice as belonging to something outside yourself, it becomes less compelling and convincing. What if you thought of it as a bad radio station? Somehow, because this voice is *inside* our head, it seems like ours and what it says seems true. If those words were coming out of someone else's mouth, what would you think of them? We're much more discriminating about what other people say to us than what we say to ourselves! So that is our spiritual work—to realize that the voice in our head has very little to do with who we are and with what will make our life work.

That voice pretends to have the answer to everything, but this is a scam. That voice has no wisdom and no good advice to offer about the things that are most meaningful to us: how to live our life, how to behave in our relationships, what choices to make and when to make them. The voice in our head has very pat answers to things. You can get nearly the same advice or answers from any ego identified person out there. The ego's advice tends to be quite predictable: Go for the money! Go for the safety! Go for the power! Take care of yourself! Watch out!

One of the biggest problems with listening to the voice in our head is that it changes its mind a lot. If you find yourself confused or changing your mind a lot, you're probably listening to this voice and not your Heart. This happens because the advice offered by the egoic mind is often based on conflicting desires. For instance, if you're thinking of traveling somewhere, one moment your mind says, "You should go. Traveling is fun," and the next moment it advises, "Don't go. It's dangerous and too expensive."

Notice that in this advice, the ego reveals some of its conflicting values: fun, safety, and money. The ego wants fun *and* safety *and* money and everything else it wants all at the same time, which is impossible. The ego can't give clear advice because many of the things the ego wants are mutually exclusive.

The ego can always come up with a reason to not follow its own advice—and it generally does! Hence, all the confusion and dissatisfaction we feel when we're living from the egoic state of consciousness. One moment the ego wants one thing, the next moment it wants something else. When we listen to the egoic mind, we are tossed to and fro by the ego's various desires.

When we let the ego's desires determine our choices and structure our lives, we often end up going in one direction and then another. At some point, we're bound to be dissatisfied with whatever we chose to do because the ego changes its mind about what it wants: We want security, so we take a job that gives us that. Then we want freedom and adventure, so we quit that job and go traveling. Then we want recognition and power, so we go back to school to get a degree. Then we discover we didn't want that degree after all. Then we want something else...

The ego's values are superficial, so following them keeps us skimming across the surface of life, never finding real meaning or fulfillment. The ego chooses to do what it does for the wrong reasons—because it wants power, respect, security, an attractive mate, a beautiful house, a perfect body, fame, popularity, and success. It wants these things because it wants to feel a certain way: It wants to feel good—it wants to be happy.

In the ego's search to feel good and to finally be at peace, it's focused on achieving future goals—it's chasing after a dream—rather than being focused on the moment-to-moment journey of life. Living a meaningful, love-filled life becomes secondary to these far-off goals. The irony is that being in the moment is where peace and happiness are actually found.

Going after such superficial goals is a recipe for not only emptiness but also corruption, as the means are often felt to justify the idealized goal. When the goal is something as superficial as the kinds of things the ego wants, the journey isn't going to be fulfilling. Even achieving those goals is bound to be a letdown because the ego can never get enough power, money, recognition, attention, or anything else. As soon as the ego gets something it wants, it wants more or something else because those things will never satisfy the longing for peace and happiness that is driving the ego. It's looking in the wrong place for peace and happiness, so how can it find them?

For our goals to be satisfying, they have to be deeper than the things the ego wants. They have to be things our Heart wants. And what one person's Heart wants is different from what another person's Heart wants, unlike all egos, which pretty much want the same things. Everyone has to find out what their own sweet Heart wants and go after that.

When we follow our Heart, the results are less important, as taking steps in alignment with our Heart is intrinsically rewarding. We are rewarded by the happiness, contentment, excitement, and joy of doing what we came here to do. And these feelings are satisfying and enough. Then if we achieve some of the results the ego wants, that's nice too—that's frosting on the cake. But the things the ego wants aren't worthwhile goals in and of themselves. They are empty and devoid of true fulfillment.

We are programmed to follow our desires. We have a desire, and we often don't question where it comes from, if it's true, or if it's worth pursuing. As with every other thought, we're programmed to believe the thought "I want" and the feelings that go with that. And when most people are pursuing these same desires, it's hard to not believe that those desires are important to our happiness and survival. Most people believe that getting what they want is the route to happiness and to surviving well, so it really seems true that if we don't get what we want we won't be happy and we might not even survive.

People are driven by fear to follow their desires. We're afraid that if we don't get what we want that will mean something terrible. The ego drives us by scaring us into thinking that getting what we want is very important—that the results are what is important, not the journey. It also drives us by using fantasies to make us believe that getting what the ego wants will be so ideal, so wonderful.

But the truth is different. Getting our ego's desires met isn't what it's cracked up to be. Getting what the ego wants isn't necessary to our happiness and it isn't particularly meaningful. For true happiness and fulfillment, we have to look somewhere other than our egoic mind because the voice in our head is clueless about what brings true happiness and meaning to life.

FEELINGS AS GUIDES

Feelings are one of the strongest determinants of what we do. They affect our behavior and choices. When the feelings stem from the ego, the choices based on them may not be very satisfying. In fact, those choices might be very poor ones, especially if they're motivated by negative feelings, such as sadness, anger, guilt, hatred, shame, fear, jealousy, and envy.

We are often encouraged to follow our feelings, but when those feelings come from the ego, look out! Such advice is most likely referring to following more positive feelings, such as joy, love, and excitement, which are signals from our Heart that a direction is right for us.

Honoring and being honest about our feelings is important. However, what often isn't understood is that honoring our feelings simply means accepting that we have them, not necessarily acting on them. People often make the mistake of thinking they have to say or do something in response to a negative feeling, or they aren't honoring that feeling. This gets people into a lot of trouble! Acting out, or even expressing, our negative feelings is rarely the best way to deal with them. It depends on *what* is wanting to act them out and express them—the ego or Essence?" It is usually the ego.

The ego creates negative feelings, and it is what wants to act them out and express them, usually in harmful ways. There are constructive ways of expressing feelings, but doing that requires getting the ego out of the way and enlisting the help of our rational, objective mind. Expressing feelings constructively is an art that most people haven't mastered. Usually expressing feelings results in letting people have it, and that can't be good for anyone.

Of the feelings that come from the ego, fear is generally the one that is most influential in our choices. When we choose out of fear, that's unfortunate. Fear is a sign of ego identification, since Essence doesn't use fear to steer us toward or away from anything. Instead, it uses joy. But the ego doesn't trust joy. Fortunately, we as humans really like joy, so we can't resist it that easily! We turn away from our joy sometimes because of fear. But when fear isn't there, joy wins out.

This is why it's so important to understand what fear is—so that it doesn't rule us and steer us away from our joy. Fear is just the ego's knee-jerk reaction to life, especially to anything or anyone new. Fear is born from the ego's belief in an imagined negative future. But how useful are these imaginations? The ego is always imagining negative possibilities because that is its job. So how can fear be a trustworthy guide for how to live our life? It can't be, but joy is. So if fear is there, notice and accept it, dismiss it, and then let joy be your guiding force.

There's one negative feeling that can come from both the ego and Essence, and that is sadness. The ego is sad often and about a lot of little things. This sadness is the result of the ego's relentless dissatisfaction with life: Nothing is ever good enough. The ego feels lacking and experiences life as lacking, and that results in ongoing disappointment and sadness. Even when things are going very well, the ego can often still find something to feel disappointed and sad about.

There is another kind of sadness. If we live in the egoic state of consciousness much of the time and follow the ego's thoughts, desires, and feelings, we may create a life that doesn't fit for us, and then we feel a deeper sadness. That deeper sadness is a message from Essence that we're out of alignment with our soul's plan. It feels like a deep and persistent longing that is calling on us to make significant changes in our life. Usually what prevents us from doing so is fear or beliefs that we cannot or should not change. Depression is often an indication of this kind of sadness.

Our other negative emotions are indications that we are believing something that isn't the whole truth, but the ego's truth, a partial truth. Shame, for instance, comes from believing we're inferior because we did something wrong, made a mistake, or are different. It comes from not being able to forgive ourselves or let go of thoughts about ourselves as flawed. Being absorbed in negative thoughts about ourselves, others, and the past results in all sorts of negative emotions, all of which are unnecessary and serve no purpose.

We don't need to feel bad! I'm not suggesting repressing or denying emotions, but not creating them in the first place by giving attention to negative thoughts and self-images. Identifying with (believing) these thoughts and images creates negative emotions. When we disidentify with negative thoughts and images (don't believe them), negative feelings aren't created.

OTHER PEOPLE AS GUIDES

If you trust the wrong things in life, like the thoughts, feelings, and desires produced by the ego, then life will show you that these things aren't trustworthy. That's how trustworthy life is! We might end up distrusting life because we trusted the wrong things, but that would be the wrong conclusion. Life is trustworthy when we put our trust in the right things, particularly our Heart.

The same could be said of people: People are trustworthy when we trust the right people. Those who operate from their ego, usually offer advice from their ego, which isn't very trustworthy, while others offer support and wisdom from Essence that is. If we trust the advice of those who aren't worthy of our trust, we're likely to make choices we regret and possibly blame life for our unhappiness. But if we put our trust in those who are worthy of it, we'll realize that life is good and supportive.

People have very different experiences of life in part because they're involved with and trust the wrong people— people who aren't so capable of loving and supporting them or of being wise. When we are children, we don't have a choice about who we're involved with. If we were assigned parents that weren't so loving or wise, we'll most likely find it difficult to trust people and trust life until we realize that the problem is that we were trusting the wrong people and that some people *are* trustworthy.

If the people we grew up around weren't worthy of our trust, we're also likely to find it difficult to trust ourselves. If we couldn't trust our parents to guide us well or love us, how can we trust our own inner guidance or trust that we are lovable? We learn to love ourselves by being loved. If someone didn't act like they loved us (even if they did), then how can we love ourselves? We trust our parents' perceptions of us, and those perceptions become our own. If we feel unloved by our parents, we assume there's something wrong with us. And if something's wrong with us, then we can't trust ourselves to be okay or for life to turn out well. And later when we realize how untrustworthy our parents were and yet we trusted them, that also makes it hard to trust ourselves, even though children can't be expected to do anything other than trust their parents.

The unfortunate thing is that if we felt unloved growing up and consequently didn't learn to love and trust ourselves, then even as an adult we tend to allow or even invite others into our lives who don't love us. Those who grew up not loving themselves don't tend to walk away from unloving and abusive people, like those who grew up loving (and trusting) themselves do. On some level, unloving people feel like a fit to those who weren't loved because unloving people make the unloved person feel like he or she did as a child. If we have an identity as inferior or a victim, we unconsciously gravitate toward those who continue to make us feel that way. To feel otherwise would feel strange, so we often remain in our familiar identity, even when that identity is painful and limiting, rather than try on a new, improved identity.

The mistake is in believing our beliefs about ourselves. An identity is just an *idea*, a thought, about ourselves and has no reality. But an identity becomes real, in a sense, once we take it on. Then others see the identity we project and react to it as if it were true, and then that identity is confirmed to us and reinforced. It becomes all the more believable. Our beliefs are often self-fulfilling prophecies.

Psychotherapy or some kind of healing work is often necessary to help people move beyond negative identities into truer and more functional ones. Limiting identities are meant to be shed once we have the resources to do so, which are available to us as adults. Taking on such identities as children is unavoidable, so there's no blame in having done this. But no one needs to keep living with self-images and beliefs that create an unhappy reality.

When we don't trust ourselves, we naturally look to others for guidance; we look outside ourselves. That's understandable, especially if we haven't learned to trust our Heart, our internal guidance system. So even those who've been misled by others may still look to others for guidance rather than follow their own inner guidance.

We might look outside ourselves for guidance because we may not be aware of our own inner guidance. We may not have learned the subtle cues or how to tune into this guidance. We also might look outside ourselves because we've gotten burned when we thought we were following our inner guidance. We might have misinterpreted what we received or took inappropriate action in response to our inner guidance.

There are some potential pitfalls in following our Heart. And one of them is that it isn't always easy to know what the Heart is saying or how to follow what it's saying. The only way to follow the Heart accurately is to be very attentive to what's coming out of the moment, moment by moment. And the egoic mind frequently interferes with that.

The trouble with looking outside ourselves for guidance is that many of the people we might look to are ego identified and unlikely to be a mouthpiece for Essence, for our own inner wisdom. If you ask advice of those who are primarily ego identified, they're likely to advise you from their ego and conditioning, which probably won't be any more helpful than the advice you'd get from your own ego and conditioning. And it probably won't fit for *you*. What do others know about your life plan and what's right for you? Even when others think they know what's right for you, do they? The trouble with taking other people's advice is that you're the one who suffers if it doesn't work out. This is one way we learn to be more discriminating about what we let guide us.

Who *can* be trusted? Can anyone? You don't really know ahead of time if someone can be trusted to give you good advice. Even a therapist or other counselor, a psychic, an astrologer, or someone else who's in the business of offering guidance might not give you the right guidance at a particular time. Guidance is very time-sensitive. What might be good general guidance could be terrible guidance for a particular person at a particular time. Even guidance from professionals could be just from their accumulated knowledge, experience, conditioning, and ego and not from Essence. Not everyone is a mouthpiece for Essence or a mouthpiece for Essence when you need them to be.

The test of how true something is for you is in how it resonates within you when you hear it. So if someone's advice doesn't ring true within your own Heart, forget it. Take what someone has to offer that does ring true and discard the rest. Your Heart is the only true guide.

Someone else in your life besides those you think of as counselors might be enlisted by Essence to be a mouthpiece of higher guidance for you. You can only know if that's the case by how that person's words feel inside you when you hear them. If someone's words make you feel relaxed, at peace, glad, joyful, and expanded, then that person is speaking the truth *for you in that moment*. If someone's words have the opposite effect, then they aren't true for you, at least not at that time.

One of the problems with psychic readings and the like is that sometimes their information isn't relevant to us right now. As much as we might like to know the future, knowing the future is highly overrated, and the future is very difficult to predict—it is hardly ever known. The most useful information and guidance is what comes out of the flow right now for where you're at right now.

Information about the future has limited value. For instance, how useful is it to be told, "I see you sitting in a large room looking out at mountains," as one psychic told me a long time ago? Since then, I've wondered which house she was referring to out of the four different houses I've lived in since then that fit that description. This information wasn't useful to me at the time or at any time, although it wasn't harmful and my ego found it tantalizing. Your own true Heart will tell you what's true and useful and what isn't.

Why are we so interested in knowing the future? One reason is that our ego would feel safer and more comfortable if we could know the future. We are also very curious creatures—we want to know what comes next in our story! Wanting to know the future is natural. Unfortunately, we don't get to know and we aren't meant to know because knowing the future might affect our choices and change our course, perhaps in ways that our course isn't meant to be changed.

There may be some things we can know and that might even be helpful to know about the future, but for the most part, the future is very fluid. There are many possible futures until one of them manifests, and then there are many possible futures again. Our future isn't set except for possibly a few predetermined events in our lifetime, but we are rarely meant to know about those events ahead of time anyway.

The more we trust life, the less we need to know the future. What will happen in the future? Exactly what needs to happen. Do we have to know what that is ahead of time if life is unfolding as it needs to? No. We only want to know what's going to happen because we don't trust life and we're afraid life won't go the way we want it to go. "Will I get what I want?" That's the question the ego most wants answered. The ego's desires cause so much suffering. It can't just relax and enjoy the ride. What if you weren't attached to life turning out a certain way? What if you trusted that life is always bringing you exactly the experience you need? That would be called happiness and peace, wouldn't it?

The ego has its ideas about how life should go and how it wants life to go. The ego's so afraid that happiness will be out of reach—or worse, great suffering will be in store—if it doesn't get what it wants in life. The funny thing and the really wonderful thing we discover is that we don't need life to be any particular way to be happy. What a relief! We can just enjoy this moment just the way it is. We might as well. This moment is all we've got. The future, in fact, doesn't exist.

WHAT GUIDES *YOUR* LIFE?

This might be a good place to do some inquiry. Here are some questions to answer that will make the information in this chapter more personally meaningful. It might be helpful to jot down the answers so that you can refer back to them some other time if you want to:

1. What are you most afraid of? What fears have been and are most prominent for you? Fear of not being loved? Fear of hurting or displeasing others? Fear of being alone? Fear of being hurt by others? Fear of not looking good? Fear of not being respected? Fear of failure? Fear of not being successful? Fear of not being able to pay your bills? Fear of living on the street? Fear of not supporting yourself? Fear of illness? Fear of mental illness? Fear of being disabled? Fear of dependency? Fear of losing your freedom? Fear of getting old? Fear of not finding meaning? Fear of not advancing spiritually? Fear of life? Fear of death?

2. How have these fears affected your choices—where you put your energy and how you spend your time? If you weren't afraid of what you're afraid of, how might you have chosen differently? How have these fears affected how you feel about life? Have they helped you in any way? How? As a result of our fears we often do develop ourselves in certain ways. For example, you might have studied hard because you were afraid you wouldn't get a good job if you didn't. Is it possible you might have developed yourself even without these fears—that you still might have studied hard or done what you needed to do anyway? What would that have been like? Our fears accompany us in life and seem to motivate us, but we don't really need fear to motivate us because Life naturally motivates us.

3. What are your ego's strongest desires (some of our desires come from Essence, not the ego)? Security? Safety? Comfort? Pleasure? Money and possessions? Beauty? Looking good? Success? Fame? Popularity? Attention? Being special? Respect and recognition? Achievement of excellence or perfection?

4. How have your ego's desires shaped your life and determined where you put your energy and how you spend your time? What percentage of your time, would you guess, goes to pursuing your ego's goals as opposed to doing what makes your Heart sing and things that drop you into Essence and feed your soul, such as just being, meditating, walking in nature, watching the sunset, enjoying loved ones, being creative, and playing and enjoying life?

5. What kinds of thoughts most commonly run through your mind? Thoughts about what you have to do and how much time you have to do it? Thoughts about other people—what you think of them and how they do things or what they think of you? Thoughts about how you or other people look? Thoughts about money? Thoughts about food? Thoughts about the past? Regrets and resentments? Thoughts about the future? Fantasies? Fears? Judgments? Opinions? "Should"s?

6. How do the thoughts that run through your mind determine how you spend your time and energy? How do they affect how you feel about life? What would your life

be like without these thoughts or if you didn't give your attention to them? These thoughts don't create a better reality for you. A better reality exists without all these thoughts. Life feels more wonderful (and more trustworthy) without such thoughts.

7. What people have most shaped your choices and your life? What guidance from others was really true for you and what wasn't? What guidance from others are you glad you followed and what guidance do you regret following?

8. What else guides your life? Can you list some instances when you feel you've been guided by life?

9. How do you experience your inner guidance? How do you know when you're being guided by your Heart? What are the signs? How has it worked out when you've followed your Heart?

WHAT GUIDES LIFE

Anyone can light a candle
But not the way that you do
Just like a flower in the wind
You are unique, the same
Each step you take, each dream you realize
Will open your Heart, your life

From the song "The Candle Song"
from *Change We Must* by Jon Anderson

Beyond and in between all the likes and dislikes of the ego and all its fears and desires is something else that guides life, but that mysterious something is much more subtle than the ego's thoughts, fears, and desires. What guides life is felt, not like emotions or sensations are felt, but more faintly than anything we sense with our senses. Still, it *is* felt, and everyone knows what it feels like because everyone has the capacity to feel the Heart, however subtle that might be. The greatest challenge in following the Heart is not in knowing what the Heart is communicating, but in acknowledging that communication and valuing and trusting it sufficiently to do its bidding.

The reason the Heart speaks to us is to bid us to do something. The Heart's communications are purposeful and meaningful. Their purpose is to move us in a direction aligned with our soul's plan, which in turn is aligned with the Whole. The Heart directs us in this dance of life to play our part, to dance our unique dance, one that no one else can do and no one else is being asked to do.

There is a plan, and that plan is discovered by listening—by being receptive—not by thinking. In each moment, all we have to do is open ourselves to receive the subtle cues within us that say, "Go this way!" All we have ever had to do is follow this voice, the voice of our true self rather than the voice in our head. Isn't it odd that we're programmed to believe that the false voice is the true one, while the true voice is so quiet, so undemanding, and so easily overlooked? We're meant to discover this about our human nature. So when the time comes, we do.

The way you can know if something you think you're receiving from the Heart—an intuition or an urge to do something—is true is that it's accompanied by a ring of truth, a sense of rightness, a "yes," a sense of "Aha!" and a sense of joy and excitement. When this "yes!" happens it's usually quite obvious.

So why do we so often have difficulty following our Heart? It's not that we don't receive the Heart's communications, but that the egoic mind talks us out of trusting and following them. It questions the Heart's communications with "buts": "But you can't do that," "But what will people say?" "But that sounds risky," "But you won't have enough money," "But you can't live like that." Our ego comes up with many of the same objections others might have if we were to tell them what our Heart wants. We are all conditioned to think the same way, to let fear and a need for safety and security rule.

It's easy to come up with reasons to not follow your Heart. That's the egoic mind's job, and it's an easy one because there are negatives to everything. But there are no good reasons to not follow your Heart. No reason is good enough. Yes, there will be challenges in following your Heart because challenges come with everything we do. But not following our Heart creates the biggest challenge of all because it goes against Life and leaves us feeling sad and lost. Of course we'll never discover the truth of this if we don't follow our Heart. We'll be left with the life the ego creates, and we'll assume that was the best we could do and perhaps the only thing we could do. We'll never know where that other path would have taken us.

If you aren't happy with your current choices, why aren't you choosing differently? What is there to lose? Is it that you don't believe happiness is possible? Are you afraid to try? Why? Are you afraid of what others will say or how they'll be affected? What are you afraid of? Do you feel you deserve to be unhappy? Can you picture yourself happy? The people who do find true happiness don't settle for unhappiness. They keep going until they find what makes them happy. They might go after what the ego wants for a while, but when that doesn't work, they try something else, like doing what they really love.

Many people don't have a model for how to be happy. If you had parents who were unhappy, you might not expect to be happy or you might not reach for happiness, and you probably weren't taught to follow your Heart. If your parents didn't follow their Heart, how could they have taught you to do that?

Those who were taught to distrust their Heart or who weren't taught to trust it have to learn this themselves. They have to find the courage within themselves to do what they weren't taught to do. That's not easy! It's difficult to go against our conditioning, even though that conditioning is negative and limiting. If we're taught something when we're young, then doing that comes naturally. If not, it's scary. So doing even what is most natural and true—following your Heart—can be very scary if you weren't taught to do that or if you were taught to do the opposite. Following our Heart is hard enough with an egoic mind that's always questioning this, but when our upbringing also doesn't support following our Heart, it's especially difficult.

To the ego, trusting the Heart feels like stepping off a cliff. The thing is, the guidance the ego offers is not safer or more certain—we just *think* it is; we are programmed to trust the egoic mind more than the Heart's subtle communications. What the mind advises *seems* safer, but that doesn't make it good advice. Advice that isn't good and isn't actually safe but just seems to be isn't very trustworthy! Good advice is also going to be safe advice, and that's what you get from the Heart—good advice that is truly safe even though it might not seem that way.

What if you trusted your Heart as much as you've trusted the egoic mind and other people's egoic minds? What choices would you make? What's good for your soul can't help but be good for others, since we are all connected and here to support each other and help each other evolve. If you aren't aligned with your plan, it isn't just you who suffers, but also those who need you to fulfill your part in the Whole.

Life doesn't seem safe, but it *is* because life is being guided by a plan devised by an Intelligence that is unimaginable to us, and yet, we are this Intelligence! No argument may be enough until you discover life's trustworthiness for yourself. You have to find out for yourself. So here's how...

WHAT TO TRUST

If the many thoughts that run through our mind can't be trusted, what can? When we stop listening to the egoic mind, it becomes clearer that something else is moving life forward, something other than our thoughts, desires, and feelings—life is happening! The ego does its part in shaping life by producing thoughts, desires, and feelings, but much more is going on in life than that. While we've been listening to the egoic mind, life has been happening: suddenly the phone rings, suddenly we speak, suddenly we jump up to do something, suddenly someone speaks to us, suddenly information comes to us, suddenly an opportunity shows up, suddenly a person shows up, suddenly love shows up, suddenly motivation to do something shows up, suddenly an "Aha" happens, suddenly we do something for someone.

When we aren't involved in our egoic mind, it's much easier to notice and appreciate how life is already happening. When we are involved in our thoughts, many of them are about what we think we need to do or should do and when. Our mind creates and implements strategies for how to make things happen in life the way we want them to happen. The ego sees itself as the main force in life, as if nothing will happen if the ego itself doesn't make it happen. Meanwhile, life is happening and bringing us the experiences, lessons, resources, information, opportunities, insights, and wisdom we need to unfold our plan.

Noticing what life is already bringing us is important because that indicates where the flow of life is going and where it wants us to go. If our ego is taking us somewhere else, we'll end up out of the flow, and we'll think that life isn't good and feel like we have to work even harder to make things turn out right. Really, we just have to join the flow wherever it is and go with it.

Something beyond us, which also *is* us, is co-creating our life with us, and it has intentions for our life—it's going somewhere. Can you think of instances when that was really obvious, when you felt carried along and everything just felt right? Life can feel this way much of the time; it doesn't have to be a struggle. Life *is* happening. It happens to us, and it also happens with our help. We tune into where the flow is going, and then we contribute our part to the flow. We co-create with what is already happening.

In order to do this, we have to be aware of what *is* happening and not be distracted by what *isn't* happening, which is primarily what the egoic mind is involved with: thoughts about the past and future, judgments, opinions, desires, fears, and other feelings. The ego lives in a parallel reality, a reality it creates mentally that has some relationship with reality but is primarily *made up*. There is reality, and then there is the egoic mind's ideas *about* reality and the feelings that are born from these ideas. These are two different realities. If we're involved in the mind's ideas about reality instead of reality, we won't be available for reality, and we may not notice how life is happening and what it wants from us.

Life is happening, but it's not happening apart from us—we are part of life happening, and we are meant to be part of it. Life needs us to participate, and we can't do that as effectively if we are lost in the clouds of our mental world. The reason that being present in the moment is so important is not just for our own peace and happiness, but because the moment needs us—Life needs us.

Each of us plays a particular role in time and space. We are like an outpost in that place in time and space for the Intelligence that we are to live through. It needs us to carry out its full vision. We are where we are and the way we are because that's what is needed. We may not be fulfilling our role completely, and often that doesn't matter, but when we're very present to life, that role can be played more completely. When we're doing our part, we feel fulfilled and content, no matter how insignificant that role might seem to be.

Being present in the moment makes it possible to play the role you came here to play. This is very important in these times, when everyone is needed to operate more from the Heart and less from the ego—because the ego has made a mess of things. This is why so many teachings today are emphasizing being in the present moment. The earth needs more of us to operate from our Heart, to align with our part in the Whole, and to overcome the pettiness and hatred the ego brings to this world.

We can't trust our minds to know what our role is in the Whole or how to play it, but we can trust our drives, our joy, and our love. What are you driven to do in this moment, or in general? What brings you joy in this moment, or in general? What do you love in this moment, or in general? These are the most important questions you can ask yourself because they hold the keys to your happiness and to what will allow you to trust life and fully serve it.

How can you trust life if you aren't happy? It's hard to conclude that life is good and trustworthy when you're not happy. The problem isn't that life isn't good or trustworthy but that you're not happy. Why? Not being happy is an indication of not being aligned with our true nature, with Essence. Happiness arrives the instant we touch into Essence, and it disappears the instant we leave Essence.

The happiness I'm talking about is not the soaring, giddy happiness the ego feels when it gets what it wants, but a much more subtle happiness. Contentment might be a better word for it. The happiness I'm talking about, which I call radical happiness, is a sense that all is right with the world and that life is precious, good, and beautiful. It's a feeling of gratitude for all of life, for the crazy, messy, and mysterious experience that it is. This is what we all really want when we say we want happiness. The ego's happiness is more like the high we get from a drug, and it can disappear just as quickly and leave us feeling let down. The happiness of being connected with our true nature, however, is the peace and contentment we have all been searching for. And it's available right now by simply being very present to this moment.

When we are very attentive to what's going on, we discover that a lot is actually going on. There probably aren't any car chases and gun battles, which the ego seems so fond of, but what *is* present is everything we need to know and everything we need to be happy. It takes directed attention, curiosity, and love to be able to appreciate the delicacy that life is, as it comes out of each moment. We have to become connoisseurs of the moment. When we give life as it is— reality—our full attention, we discover just how marvelous, mysterious, rich, and meaningful it is. All that's required is our full attention and curiosity: What's happening *now?*

What we discover is that quite a lot is happening, including things we didn't know were going to happen. Being present in the moment is a place of receptivity, wonder, curiosity, and joy in discovery. What will happen next? What happens comes in many forms: motivation happens, urges to do something happen, thoughts happen (but we don't have to get lost in them), sensations happen, sounds happen, seeing happens, things happen in the environment, intuition and insights pop into our mind. The more we give our attention to the things that are coming out of the moment instead of getting lost in the virtual reality of our thoughts, the more we'll begin to live from Essence and be Essence in the world and fulfill Essence's plan.

Living from Essence instead of the ego is largely a matter of moving our attention to reality and away from what is not real: thoughts, feelings, and desires. The ego's virtual reality is part of reality, but when we make it our entire reality, we suffer. When we're in touch with reality, we feel happy, and life feels good and trustworthy. Once we discover the secret to being happy, life is much easier to trust. And that secret is to be in the moment, give your attention to what's real, and let the motivation, joy, and love that come out of the moment naturally move you in life.

Let your motivation, joy, and love be your guide. In every moment, they are guiding you. You have the free will to choose whether they guide you or your egoic mind guides you. These are mutually exclusive choices, different ways of living and being that lead to different experiences of life. Can you trust

enough to let your own inner wisdom, your own sweet Self
guide you?

CHAPTER 5
Developing Trust

TRUST IS DEVELOPED BY BEING PRESENT

Trust in life is something that is developed. We don't become trusting of life all of a sudden, when before we weren't. Trust is something that takes time to develop. It requires practicing giving attention to what is true and real in the moment rather than to what is less true and real—our thoughts, particularly our fears and doubts.

The reason we feel fearful and distrust life is we're trusting the egoic mind; we're identifying with it and agreeing with its perception of danger everywhere. This is natural, but it results in believing a lie—that our fears and doubts are meaningful representations of reality. We often have to see the truth again and again—that our fears and doubts are not valuable and helpful guides to life—before our attachment to the egoic mind is lessened.

So the development of trust is closely tied to our spiritual evolution, which is toward living in Essence and trust and away from ego identification and fear. The Catch-22 is that believing the ego's fears and doubts keeps us identified with the ego and unable to experience the truth—that life is trustworthy and that we can trust being in the moment without all of our egoic mind's thoughts. It really is safe to not think those thoughts! But how will we find this out if we don't give being in the moment a try? We all experience being present briefly throughout our day, but often our mind snatches us out of the moment before Presence has a chance to affect us.

The trouble, again, is the ego. The ego doesn't like to be in the moment and resists being present because the ego, the sense of being someone, disappears when we are absorbed in the moment, when we're lost in whatever we're doing or in whatever's going on. Who can blame the ego?

So what can you do? The solution is to accept that your ego doesn't want to be in the moment and not let that stop you from practicing being more present. You see, there's something else here that *does* want to be in the moment, but it isn't as insistent or attention-getting as the ego.

Can you find the *you* that wants to be in the moment and enjoys it? That's who you really are, and the resistant part of you is just the ego, the false self. Just let the ego be there and let it be resistant, like a rebellious child, while you firmly commit to being present. Become really familiar with your dual nature. Learn to recognize the ego when it shows up. Learn to see it as programming and not who you really are. Then notice what else is here besides the ego, besides that resistance.

The ego's responses to life don't have to be yours. You have a choice once you see that there is one: You can listen to the egoic mind—the voice of the ego—or not. What is it that can choose? This is the great mystery. Who you really are is a great mystery! It is called Awareness by many because that's one thing you can say about it—it's aware. Who you really are is what's aware of your thoughts and everything else. It's not only aware, but also capable of evaluating and being objective about thoughts.

Our thoughts seem so true. We automatically believe them and aren't very objective about them. But something else is capable of being objective. It's funny how easily we can analyze, evaluate, and be objective about other people's thoughts, but we don't necessarily apply the same objectivity and analysis to our own. That's no mistake. This is the programming that keeps what mystics call the Illusion in place. Once we apply that same objectivity to our own thoughts, the Illusion falls apart. The false self can't be maintained.

The spiritual path, which has traditionally used meditation, inquiry, and other spiritual practices to realize this great truth, is quite simply about recognizing that who we *think* we are isn't who we really are. Rather, we are what notices thinking. We are the Noticer.

But this Noticer is not just an observer of life, but also participating in this grand play. We (as Oneness) are playing the role of all the characters, even though it seems that we are a particular character. We (as Oneness) are looking through every set of eyes, even though it seems we have just one pair of eyes. What all the eyes see isn't registering in each individual, but it's registering in the Oneness to which we belong. We experience having only one set of eyes, but what is looking through these eyes is the same thing that looks through every pair of eyes. That is who we really are.

Once we get a taste of this Noticer, it becomes easier to not believe our thoughts, to disidentify from the egoic mind and the ego's drives, desires, doubts, and fears. The ego begins to lose its hold on us. And yet, most people don't experience a complete and instantaneous dropping away of the ego. More often, disidentification happens slowly and parallels the development of trust.

Those who've had their trust damaged as children are at a disadvantage because the ego's ordinary amount of distrust is magnified and may seem insurmountable. The fear and doubt can be very, very strong and consequently very convincing. But how convincing a thought is, is not the measure of its truth.

Thoughts that belong to our programming were meant to be convincing. That was built into such thoughts. Without the ability to make thoughts convincing, the Oneness could not have created a false self. It couldn't have the experience of being a unique individual having a human experience. It couldn't have gotten lost in its human creations.

People who have awakened out of this programming know this. They know who they really are, and they know what it's like to be lost in identification with the false self. And they know the way out. There have always been individuals who have known the way out. The Oneness has given us individuals who can show the way because we're meant to find the way out too. It is a perfect plan. The false self is no mistake. It serves until it no longer serves, and then we begin to hear the call to wake up and discover who we really are.

Practice: Getting to Know Yourself as Awareness/Aliveness

Who you are is Awareness. You are what is aware of whatever you are aware of. You are aware of reading these words right now. How do you experience that Awareness? Does it have an energetic feel to it? Some call Awareness "aliveness" or "awakeness" because it feels alive and awake.

When we are in our body and senses and not in our head, we experience a sense of aliveness that is felt as a subtle energetic vibration, or tingling, and a sense of being alive, illumined, bright, and aware. These sensations are how who we really are is experienced by the body-mind. That aliveness is the felt-sense of who we really are and what we experience when we are in the Now. When we're aligned with who we really are and not identified with the ego, we feel that aliveness energetically, and it feels good.

Take a moment to experience this aliveness, which is also called Presence. It's often easiest to experience it in the hands, so take a moment to notice the sensations in your hands. You can do this with your eyes open or closed. Can you sense a tingling, alive, vibration in your hands? It's more subtle than the usual sensations, but still there. Just stay with these sensations for a moment. Become familiar with them.

These sensations of aliveness can actually be felt in any part of your body. So now move your awareness to your arms. Are you able to feel the aliveness there too? What about in your feet? Your legs? Your torso? Your neck? Your head?

Whenever you find yourself caught up in your egoic mind and ego, you can use this sense of aliveness to bring you back into the Now simply by tuning in to the aliveness.

Inquiries for Experiencing Who You Are

1. <u>Take some time to examine what you are referring to when you think the thought "I."</u> Try to find the *I* you're referring to when you're thinking about yourself. Can you locate it anywhere? You may point to your body when you say "I," but the *I* isn't just the body is it? Does the *I* reside in the body? If it resides in the body, what is it that's aware of your body and your thoughts and even able to contemplate this question? Could that awareness be who you really are? Is awareness—consciousness—limited to the body or the mind? What if you were that awareness, and you were just pretending to be attached to a particular body-mind for the experience it provides consciousness? Who would you be then?

   The real you is not your body, your mind, your personality, or any of the things you call yourself, anything that might come after the words "I am." What are such labels, after all? They are just ideas, concepts. Are you an idea, or are you what is *aware* of the ideas, labels, thoughts, desires, and feelings of a particular body-mind?

2. <u>What are you aware of right now?</u> If you are aware of a thought, ask: "Who or what is aware of this thought?" If you are aware of a feeling, ask: "Who or what is aware of

this feeling?" If you are aware of a sensation, ask: "Who or what is aware of this sensation?" Take sufficient time with each of these questions to allow yourself to experience what is aware of a thought, feeling, or sensation.

The real you is what is aware of every thought, feeling, sound, sensation, intuition, urge, and insight—everything you are aware of. You are what is experiencing this life, and that has no gender, age, past, future, or any other specific definition, but is pure Awareness, Consciousness. Who is it that is aware of the thoughts that seem to define you? Is it the character you seem to be, or is there something else here that is character-less, that is just purely experiencing life, without ideas about liking or disliking, having or not having, wanting or not wanting?

MEDITATION

Leaving the ego and its fears and doubts behind is more difficult if we haven't had experiences of who we really are. If we aren't very familiar with Essence, then we don't know what will take the place of the egoic mind. What will guide us if not our thoughts? Many people get that they aren't the ego or the mind, but they haven't realized who they really are fully enough to be willing to move out of their egoic mind for very long. Where would they go? The ego tells them there's nothing else and that the present moment is boring, and when they look, what's beyond the ego seems like a void, like nothing.

Who we really are can feel pretty empty and insubstantial and therefore scary when we haven't had a fuller experience of it. That Nothingness, which is often how the ego experiences the Now, can make disidentifying with the ego frightening until we come to see that something very trustworthy is living our life.

So for most people, moving from the ego to Essence is a gradual process, one of dipping their toe into Essence, or the Now, running back to the egoic mind, and then back to Essence. Eventually we stay longer in the Now, long enough to begin to trust it. At a certain point, we're ready to take the leap and leave the egoic mind behind, but only after we've had enough experiences of Essence to see that Essence exists and is worthy of our trust.

Meditation is the most powerful tool for learning to be more present, for learning to live more from our natural state, from the Noticer, or Essence. This is why meditation has been recommended as a spiritual practice for centuries. If you want to overcome your fears and become more trusting of life, meditation will help you do that like nothing else can.

Meditation is, very simply, taking time to practice being present. Meditation quiets the mind, which enables us to experience what Essence is like. Meditation shows us what else is possible besides our constricted, limiting, and fearful identities. Spiritual experiences and altered states of consciousness do this as well. By giving us a taste of Essence, meditation fuels our will and strengthens our commitment to breaking free from the egoic state of consciousness.

How to Meditate

Meditation is actually very simple, very enjoyable—and it will change your life. You don't need to sit any particular way or breathe any particular way, unless you want to. Sitting up straight is recommended, but you don't have to do that to benefit from meditation. You don't even have to have a special place to meditate, although sitting in the same place at the same time each day can be conducive to a practice of meditation. All you need is a quiet place where you can go and not be disturbed for a while.

The more rules and hurdles you create around meditating, the more likely your mind will talk you out of it. So make meditation as easy and as comfortable as possible to ensure that you actually do it.

This goes for the kind of meditation you do as well: Meditate in the way that you most enjoy and works best for you. This may seem obvious, but sometimes people force themselves to follow certain techniques because a book or someone they know says that's the way to do it. Meditation doesn't have to be complicated or difficult. Find a way to do it that you enjoy so that you'll want to do it every day.

The purpose of meditation is to quiet the mind so that we can experience what else is here besides our thoughts. The mind can be quieted by focusing on any number of things, which accounts for the various types of meditation. Usually, focusing on the breath or a sensory experience is suggested. Both the breath and the senses are doorways into the Now, or Stillness.

When we focus on the breath or a sight, sound, or physical or energetic sensation, the mind is quieted because we can't think and fully sense at the same time. For instance, you can't simultaneously listen to what someone is saying and think. Similarly, you can't be fully absorbed in listening (meditating) to a piece of music and think. The same is true of any sense: If you're fully engaged in sensing something, that precludes thinking. If you are thinking while you're sensing something, you aren't fully sensing it, although you might still be aware of it.

The goal in meditation is to be fully engaged in sensing and not in thinking. So the simplest instruction for meditation is to be fully engaged with whatever you are sensing (including your breath), and whenever your mind wanders from that, gently bring it back to sensing.

You can meditate (focus) on music. Or you can meditate on the sounds in your environment and on the silence in between those sounds. Or you can meditate on a beautiful flower, a sunset, the breeze blowing through the trees, the clouds moving across the sky, or any other beautiful sight that has the capacity to capture your attention. Or you can meditate to the physical and energetic sensations in your body as you're sitting or moving. Tai Chi, Qigong, yoga, and other body-oriented spiritual practices have you focus on the body and the sensations related to positions and movements of the body. Focusing on the breath and the sensations involved in breathing is the most basic and common meditation suggested by spiritual traditions. Focusing on anything other than thoughts puts you in a meditative state.

Different people enjoy different types of meditations. I'm very auditory and find it easy and enjoyable to meditate to music, and I'm not very body-oriented, so practices like yoga are less appealing to me. Experiment and find out what you most enjoy focusing on. The simple instruction, once again, is to put your attention on what you're listening to, watching, or sensing in some other way, and when you catch yourself thinking, bring your attention back to just sensing.

Of course, you can also focus on what's coming into all of your senses all at once. This is a good way to stay anchored in the Now as you go about your day. During your day, make it a habit to pay attention to what you are sensing rather than to what you're thinking. The result of being more in your body and senses during the day is peace, contentment, happiness—and effectiveness. Listening to our thoughts often distracts us from what we're doing and makes us less effective, not just less happy.

How Long to Meditate

Meditating for a half hour a day is a good place to start, although an hour a day will really make a difference in your life. If a half hour is all you can do, then do that, but do it every day at least once a day. Regularity is very important. We practice being identified with the mind every day, so it makes sense that we also need to practice *dis*identifying with the mind every day.

The reason for meditating at least a half hour is that when you first start meditating, it will probably take that long to move out of the mind and into a quieter, more peaceful state, which is the reward of meditating. If you meditate for only fifteen minutes, your mind may still be as busy as when you started, and you might not get to the point where meditation feels worthwhile. You may have to stay with meditation at least a half hour a day for a while before it begins to be rewarding, pleasurable, and easy. But it will be worth the commitment.

There are many things we do that aren't easy, but we do them for the long-term benefits. Like many other things, meditation gets easier after you've practiced it a while. The longer you practice meditation and the more time you spend in meditation, the more established you'll become in the Now, and the easier it will be to be in the Now during your day.

What follows are some practices, inquiries, and specific meditations for you to do to help you develop your ability to be present and experience Essence:

Inquiries About Meditation

1. <u>Take some time to examine any resistance you may have to meditating.</u> How do you (your ego) feel about meditating regularly? How do your thoughts and beliefs about meditating keep you from meditating? And when you are meditating, what thoughts come up to try to take you away from meditating or discourage you from continuing? You don't have to respond to these thoughts. They aren't really your thoughts, but your ego's thoughts. Recognize them as ploys on the part of the ego to get you to pay attention to

the mind and not meditate. You are what is aware of the thoughts going through your mind.

2. Do you believe meditation is valuable? If not, how do you convince yourself that it isn't? If you don't believe meditation is valuable, then you probably won't do it. What do you value? We tend to take time for what we value. Given that, what does what you do with your time and energy say about what you value? Does what you spend your time doing reflect what you really want?

    Notice how the mind devalues meditation. Notice how else the mind might undermine your commitment to becoming freer, happier, and more trusting of life. The mind often drives us in directions that aren't worthy of our time and energy with "should"s, guilt, fear, and desire.

Practices Related to Meditation

1. Notice how uninterested the mind is in the present moment. The mind is fascinated with the past and the future, and it likes to evaluate the present, but the mind finds nothing of interest in the actual experience of the moment. Notice how persistently your mind makes suggestions for thinking about something or doing something other than just being in the moment and responding to whatever is coming out of the moment. The mind has a job to do, and that job is to keep you out of the Now.

How does your mind attempt to keep you out of the moment? Which tactics are the most successful at getting you to turn away from being in the moment? A memory? A fantasy? A desire? A fear? A should? A judgment? A thought about food, sex, time, work, what you have to do, imperfection, cleanliness, being successful, or how you look? How long do you actually stay in the Now before you go unconscious and rejoin the egoic mind?

2. Notice what's coming out of the Now: As you go about your day, notice what's arising in the Now. Is the ego saying no to that, complaining about it? That could be one of the things happening in the present moment. What else is happening? What sensations? What sounds? What are you seeing? What intuitions? What inspirations? What urges? What drives? What impressions? What judgments? What feelings? What desires? What fears? What are you experiencing? Tension? Stress? Relaxation? Contraction? Expansion? Awareness? Presence? Silence? Acceptance? Beauty? Love? Joy? Peace?

Any number of these things could be coming out of the Now. Something is always arising, and something is always being taken in by you. What's happening right now? Notice how the egoic mind tries to co-opt the moment and draw you into being absorbed in thinking again. The egoic mind especially likes to think about the past, the future, what it likes and doesn't like, what there is to do, and other people. When you catch yourself thinking, bring your awareness back to your sensory experience and to everything else that's coming out of the Now.

Just experience everything you're experiencing without labeling or evaluating it. Let the moment be as it is. You'll discover that action also comes out of the Now, spontaneously and easily. You naturally do what you need to do. You don't need your thoughts to impel you.

3. Experiment with using beauty as a doorway into the Now. Beauty brings us into the Now. When you notice something beautiful, how does it make you feel? It opens your Heart, doesn't it? This is the experience of Essence. You can always find your way back to Essence by noticing something beautiful. Make noticing beauty and spending some time with beauty part of your daily practice. Here are some ways to do that:

Choose something beautiful to look at. Give it your full attention. If evaluations, labels, or other thoughts come up about what you're looking at or about anything else, gently bring your attention back to just seeing. Receive the visual impression and experience its impact on your being. How does the experience of seeing without thinking feel energetically? That peace and contentment is who you are!

Alternately, move your gaze from object to object, without letting it rest on any one thing. This is an especially good practice for when you are walking in nature. Keep your eyes moving around your environment. If thoughts arise about what you're seeing or about anything else, notice them, and then go back to seeing and experiencing the impact beauty has on you energetically.

Meditations

Here are a few different kinds of meditations to try out on your own to help you discover how you might enjoy meditating:

<u>On sound:</u> Listen to the sounds around you. Receive the sounds without mentally commenting on them. If you catch yourself thinking, bring yourself back to listening. If you find yourself resisting a sound, such as a barking dog, notice that resistance and then bring yourself back to listening.

Alternately, listen to the silence in between the sounds and in between the thoughts. What do you experience energetically? If you catch yourself describing what you're experiencing mentally or thinking about something else, notice that and then return to the experience of silence. Stay with this experience a while without rushing off to do something else or follow a thought. Notice how pleasurable just listening is. That experience is who you are!

<u>On your breath:</u> Notice the experience of breathing. Notice the feel of the breath as it enters your nose and leaves your nose. Without changing how you breathe in any way, notice how the body breathes rhythmically in and out, effortlessly, softly, gently—and there you are in the Now. If you find yourself thinking about your breathing, your body, or anything

else, bring your attention back to the experience of breathing. The more you practice this, the easier it becomes to move into the Now, and the more you'll want to.

On all your senses: What's coming in through your senses right now? What are you experiencing? A sound? A sight? Something touching you? Warmth? Coolness? Air moving? Tension? Pain? Pleasure? Many sensations are likely to be happening at once. Notice them without labeling them, evaluating them, or thinking about them. If you find your mind doing that, bring your attention back to the experience your senses are bringing you. Experience whatever you're experiencing without judging it or trying to hold on to it or push it away. Let it be the way it is. Experience what it's like to be a receptor. How does that feel energetically?

A Guided Meditation for Being Present

Here is a guided meditation that you can record for yourself to listen to daily or at least a few times a week to help you be more present:

Get very comfortable and relax into whatever position you are in, with your eyes open or closed. This is your special time, so set aside all thoughts, worries, concerns, and to-do lists and just be. Just be here right now without any of that. You don't need these thoughts, and you have never needed them to be who you are and to do what you came here to do. That which you truly are is right here, right now taking care of everything that needs taking care of. Right now, it's time to just be and to discover what just being is like. By just being still and letting go of any thoughts and concerns, you can discover what your true nature is like and what it's like to live as that. You may think you need your thoughts to be and to survive, but they only interfere with being and with becoming what you can be.

Sink down deeper into whatever position you are in and just notice whatever you are aware of. As you listen to these words, notice the effect they have on you... Notice how your body feels... how your being feels... how this experience feels...

As you continue to allow yourself to experience what you are experiencing, notice whatever else you are experiencing...

Now, with your eyes open, notice the beauty that exists in this moment. How is beauty showing itself to you in this moment? Take a moment to take in whatever beauty you are noticing...

Once again, just notice the experience of you being here now in this moment... Notice how the body feels... Notice how your being feels... Notice how this unique moment in time feels... If a thought comes in, then notice that and then go back to noticing what else is present here in this moment. There's actually a great deal to be aware of, a great deal of richness, beauty, uniqueness, a great deal to be grateful for... If gratitude is coming up, then notice that and continue to notice everything else that's part of this moment. Take some time to just experience, as if you had never seen or heard or been alive before in this world...

Continue to move your attention around, just noticing all that you can notice, just touching that experience and then noticing what else is here. Your mind might want to tell a story or comment about or judge what you're noticing because that's what minds do. When that's happening, just notice that. Thoughts are part of experience, but they are just a small part of experience—and not very true. They're stories we tell ourselves about experience, but they lack the richness and aliveness of the real experience, of really experiencing life. Continue now to just notice and experience whatever you are noticing and experiencing for as long as you like.

OVERCOMING FEAR AND DOUBT

While fear grabs our attention and yanks us out of the Now, doubt acts more subtly, but has the same effect. While fear is a voice of alarm, doubt is quite another kind of voice. Doubt sounds reasonable and rational, like sound advice, while actually being infused with fear: "You might get hurt. It's risky. It might not work out." The voice of doubt is a voice we've all heard countless times from parents and others in our lives who have our best interests in mind but are actually operating out of fear.

Doubt keeps us from following our Heart just as effectively as fear. Doubt cracks the door open to the unknown negative possibility. It is the "yes but" that takes the wind out of our sails and throws water on our fire. It often takes the form of self-doubt: "I probably won't get that job anyway (so why apply?)." However, more generalized doubt, or distrust in life, can be equally paralyzing: "Nothing I do matters anyway (so why try?)."

A doubt is actually a disguised fear. It's the fear that things won't turn out, that something isn't worth doing, that life isn't good or worth living, or that we aren't good enough. It is belief in the negative. While fear is the belief in a specific negative outcome, doubt is the belief in the *possibility* of a negative outcome. Fear is a doubt that has crystallized into a more specific imagined picture, while doubt is more vague, which makes doubt more insidious than fear because doubt is more difficult to refute. With doubt, you aren't sure what might go wrong, but you believe something will. And you're probably right! You probably will run into difficulties, and there will be things you won't like—because that's life. The question is, will that stop you from following your Heart?

Doubts are stoppers. They stop us from doing what we feel moved to do, what our Heart calls us to do. Because doubts come from the ego, not from the Heart, they aren't true warnings that should be heeded. Doubts are the programmed, automatic response of the ego to life: "You better watch out. Life is dangerous. You'll fail. You'll end up homeless." Our ego and other people's egos spew out the same responses to change or to trying something new. Such doubts are quite predictable. They're programmed into every mind. When faced with the unknown, out come the doubts.

Because doubts come at us from both inside and outside ourselves, they seem believable. If everyone has similar doubts, we assume these doubts must have some validity. We assume there must be something to be concerned about. Fear is contagious—it activates fear in others. The egoic state of consciousness brings out the egoic state of consciousness in others. And all egos agree: The world is a scary and unsafe place. Egos are happy to recount stories of all the terrible things that have happened to them and to others.

Buying into such unspecified fears has kept many people from following their Heart and living the life they were meant to live. Life can be scary, and challenging things happen sometimes. But such things happen whether we follow our Heart or not, so we might as well follow our Heart.

A Guided Meditation for Being with Fear

Below is a guided meditation for you to record and listen to that will help you be with your fear or any other difficult feeling in a way that will release and heal it. This is a way of working with a feeling that simply allows it and accepts it without repressing it, feeding it, expressing it, or acting it out, which are all the things we tend to do with uncomfortable feelings. A feeling is healed by bringing awareness and acceptance to it, by just letting it be here without doing anything about it. Thinking about feelings, acting them out, and expressing them only strengthen feelings and ensure that they'll keep coming up. Some feelings will need to be sat with again and again in the following way before everything is seen that needs to be seen:

Recall a time recently when a fear or other difficult feeling grabbed you. Just recall it without thinking any more about it or getting involved in it. We are going to take some time to get to know this feeling and what's behind it, so all you need to do right now is recall a time when you had a feeling that you'd like to explore further. Take a minute to call that up from your memory...

Every feeling has a certain energy, or feel, to it. Can you sense the energy of this feeling? What is it like? What does it feel like?... Do you

experience it in a particular area of your body?... Does it have a color?...
A size?... Just sit with the energy of this feeling a while, like a guest who's
come to visit that you're just getting to know. Welcome and give space to
this guest. Be curious about this feeling. Your true self–Essence–is what is
able to sit with, notice, and accept the feeling. And from Essence, feelings
can be healed. So just allow the energy to be here and experience it fully.

All that feelings really want and need is our attention, and then they
will relax. Like an upset child, our feelings just need to be attended to
before they quiet down. So, let's just be very quiet and listen to this feeling,
and see what happens and if there's something we can learn about it.
Feelings have a gift to offer us–a gift of information. They have something
to tell us about our thoughts. We aren't going to analyze this feeling with
our minds, but set the mind aside and just listen, like a parent would just
hold a child and listen to him or her. We are listening with our intuition,
our Heart, not our mind. So, let's take some time to do this. What we
especially want to know is what thoughts or beliefs led to this feeling,
what is behind it?

Practices for Overcoming Fear and Doubt

1. <u>Notice when fear is triggered.</u> During your day, when fear
   comes up, take a moment and examine where it came from
   and its validity. Fear comes from a thought, not something
   objective, not reality, but a supposition about what might
   happen in the future. What thoughts or images do you
   think created the fear you are feeling? They could be from
   someone else, including from TV or a movie, not just your
   own thoughts. Are these thoughts based in reality, that is,

are they true *now?* Is there a current threat that needs to be responded to?

Uncovering the thoughts, beliefs, and images behind a fear will diffuse its power—if you also see that these thoughts aren't true. Only when we believe these thoughts do they have the power to frighten us. If you don't believe a scary thought, it won't scare you. So discovering the thoughts behind the fear and then seeing that those thoughts have no basis in reality here and now is key in becoming free from needless fear, which saps our energy and joy for life. Such thoughts are not just untrue but dysfunctional, since they have no power to protect us from what we fear. So why give your attention to them?

When something actually happens in our life that is potentially frightening, like an accident, we deal with it in the moment, and there often isn't even time to be afraid. Fear is the result of believing scary thoughts and not being present in the moment. The present moment contains resources for dealing with whatever challenges we may face.

2. Notice the voice of doubt. As you go about your day, notice your thoughts that express doubt. Notice how reasonable this voice sounds, how wise and convincing it sounds. This voice may seem wise, but notice that it comes up regularly and predictably: As soon as a choice needs to be made or soon after one is made, there it is. This voice questions automatically, and its questioning isn't based on wisdom, but programming. The mind is programmed to

doubt. Doubts are one of the ego's automatic responses to life.

If you need to be careful and you're in the Now, you'll be careful, and the choices you make will be wise. You don't need the doubting mind to take care of you. Doubts only confuse us and cause us to make poor decisions. Doubtful thoughts are easy to come by and not necessarily wise.

3. Notice all the ways that life supports your life. As you go about your day, notice how supportive life is. It has provided a world, a nation, a community, family, friends, and others that help you survive and provide what you need. What a miracle! What other grace and support do you experience in your life? What are you grateful for? Focusing on what you *have*, instead of on what you don't have, what you want, or what you might not have in the future, helps you be in the moment and experience the goodness and trustworthiness of life.

Inquiries for Overcoming Fear and Doubt

1. What kinds of doubts do you experience? Do you doubt yourself? Do you doubt others? Do you doubt life? Distrust is at the bottom of doubt. Do you distrust yourself—your choices? Do you distrust others? Do you distrust life? What form do your doubts come in? Do you doubt that you will be okay in the future? That's the most common doubt.

Our doubts are all trying to second-guess the future, which is impossible. We doubt our choices because we're trying to make the "right" choice for the future, but the mind will never know what is right for us. Only the Heart knows, and the Heart doesn't communicate through thoughts such as doubts.

2. <u>How do you distrust life?</u> Do you distrust that you'll be able to provide for yourself or that life will provide the financial and material support you need? Is there evidence for life not supplying what you need? Life doesn't always give us what we want, but that doesn't mean it doesn't give us what we need.

Do you distrust that you'll have a happy life? Many people believe that happiness is for other people, not for them, especially if they've had an unhappy childhood. This is a mistaken belief that needs to be seen, as it can be a self-fulfilling prophecy, like so many negative beliefs. Happiness is available to everyone because happiness comes from the attitude we bring to life, not what life brings to us.

Do you distrust that you will find love? That's impossible, since love is yours to give, and it is in giving love that we feel love, not in being loved.

Do you distrust that you will be safe from harm? It's true that our bodies can be harmed, and this is part of life. But who we really are can never be harmed, and the love and wisdom that we are is always available even when the body has been harmed. Love, happiness, and peace are even available when the body no longer functions well, and sometimes that's exactly what we're meant to discover when something happens to the body. Nothing, in fact, can interfere with our capacity to love, be happy, and be at peace except how we think about whatever life brings us. This is really good news.

3. <u>What evidence do you have that life is trustworthy?</u> List some instances when life has been supportive without a lot of effort on your part—when life just brought you the job, person, opportunity, money, thing, free time, friendship, love, kindness, information, guidance, or support you needed just when you needed it. It's very important to acknowledge the goodness, support, and grace that does exist in our lives because the ego tends to overlook this and focus on what it wants to have happen, not what is happening that's supportive right here and now. The ego often takes for granted the support that we do have.

    The more you notice how life is supporting and has supported you, the easier it will be to relax, move out of the egoic mind, and enjoy the adventure that this life is. It will be the adventure it is, so you might as well enjoy it! The mind thinks it can make life be other than it is by thinking about it, wishing, dreaming, desiring, and complaining. But life is the way it is for now. Can you enjoy it just the way it is for now, for this unique moment and these unique circumstances will never come again? Can you trust that whatever experience you've having right now is the right one for now?

WORKING WITH THE INNER CHILD

If your trust has been damaged in childhood, it will be important to do some inquiry and other kinds of healing work around this to help restore trust. One of the most effective healing methods is Inner Child work. It's designed to heal the erroneous and usually damaging conclusions we came to as a child as a result of our upbringing and other experiences.

The child we once were lives on within us in our unconscious and is called the Inner Child. If our Inner Child's healthy development was impeded or arrested, we can help her (or him) grow up by meeting with her in our imagination and giving her what she needed that she didn't get. We can be the loving and wise parent she needed but may not have had and thereby heal any wounding that occurred.

When we do this work in our imagination, an amazing thing happens: The child who once felt unloved, unhappy, and distrustful is transformed into a child who feels loved, happy, and trusting, and then that becomes the state in which she lives on in our unconscious.

The effect is that a happy Inner Child won't sabotage us with negativity, fears, and doubts like an unhappy Inner Child. Many of the negative thoughts, fears, and doubts that arise in our egoic mind come from our Inner Child. When she is healed, those thoughts either disappear altogether or aren't as compelling and can be dismissed more easily.

The reason working with the Inner Child through our imagination—through images—is effective is that our memories of our childhood are stored as images, and they affect us subconsciously. When we bring these images into consciousness and work with them in our imagination, they're re-stored as new images, replacing the old ones, which effectively reprograms the unconscious. Since psychological complexes like the Inner Child are stored as images and can be accessed through the imagination, it makes sense that they can be worked with and reprogrammed through the imagination as well. Hypnotherapy works with imagery in a similar way to heal traumas and transform behaviors.

Many find they can do Inner Child work easily and safely enough on your own, although you might want to find a therapist to help you, especially if you experienced a lot of abuse as a child or if you're experiencing intense or overwhelming feelings.

To prepare to do this work, sit or lie down in a comfortable position, relax, take some time to move into a peaceful state, and affirm your willingness and readiness to receive the understanding and healing you need.

When you're ready to begin, invite your Inner Child to come forward so that you can interact with her (or him) and get to know her. Doing this work doesn't take any special skill or talent. Most people can see their Inner Child in their imagination quite easily. Can you see her in your mind's eye? What does she look like? How old is she? What is she wearing?

Your Inner Child is not an idea of yourself but a psychological complex that exists within you. When you call her forth, this complex is what you experience, not just an idea of what you were like as a child. Working with your Inner

Child is not carried out on a mental level but on a psychic level.

The communication you will have with your Inner Child is a sacred one, as it is a precious opportunity to connect with an aspect of yourself that has a powerful influence on how you feel about yourself and how you operate in life. It's an opportunity to find out what conclusions she came to as a result of her experiences and how those conclusions have been influencing your feelings and behavior as an adult. It's also an opportunity to comfort and heal the Inner Child and, in so doing, heal yourself.

As part of getting to know your Inner Child, you'll have a dialogue with her. You'll ask her some questions about herself and then listen for her answers, which will come to you intuitively. When we invite material to arise from the unconscious and give it space to be received, something will show up that's pertinent to the inquiry. Dialoging in this way requires receptivity on our part—not thinking. So for the time being, do your best to set the thinking mind aside.

One of the most important things you want to explore with your Inner Child is what it's like to be her: How does she feel about herself? Her parents? Her friends? Life? The Future?

The answers to these questions will give you a good idea of what she believes—what she's concluded—about herself, other people, and life. For instance, if she says she feels lost and alone, what might she have concluded about herself, life, and others? Any number of conclusions are possible.

These conclusions are something for you to explore later through inquiry: What conclusions did your Inner Child come to as a result of feeling the way she felt or having the experiences she had? These conclusions continue to have some influence on us as an adult, particularly if we are unaware of them. Awareness frees us from them to a great extent.

After getting to know your Inner Child some, the next step is to ask her what she needs and wants from you. And then tell her the things she needs to hear, the things a wise and loving parent would say to her. Be that loving, wise, and compassionate parent that she and every child deserves. Tell her things like: you love her and you see what a beautiful child she is, what happened to her wasn't fair, it wasn't her fault, she didn't deserve it, she is strong and courageous to have survived, she was just doing what children do, she did the best she could to take care of herself, she is lovable and capable, she is full of goodness, she deserves to be happy, she can trust life.

Tell her all the things she needs to hear so that she can relax and be happy and at peace. What will make her feel loved, happy, trusting, and at peace with herself and with life? Whatever it is that has this effect is the truth. The conclusions she came to that made her feel the opposite weren't true. They were misunderstandings on her part—the understandable but wrong conclusions that children often come to. Help her see things more clearly and truly. Help her see the truth about herself, about her parents, about life, about other people. You have the wisdom within you now to see things from another perspective, from the perspective of an adult.

Sit her on your lap, hold her, comfort her, stroke her hair in the way you would like to have been held and cared for as a child. Give her the attention, love, affection that she needed. Be the ideal parent that she didn't have.

When this exchange feels finished, tell your Inner Child you'll be back soon to spend some time with her again. And be sure to do that, even if it's just a few minutes. Establish a relationship with your Inner Child. When you're upset about something, visit with her and see what she might have to say about it. See what you can learn from her about why you feel the way you do.

Inquiries to Free Yourself from Negative Beliefs

1. Make a list of negative beliefs you hold about yourself, life, and others. Counteract each belief with a positive statement or statements—something Essence might say instead. Be your own wise healer by responding to your negative beliefs with the kindness, compassion, and wisdom of Essence. Doing this will help neutralize a negative belief and any feelings attached to it. Repeat this exercise whenever a negative belief arises, especially when there are strong feelings attached to it.

2. Notice how you are able to ignore some negative thoughts and not others. Why is that? The thoughts that are difficult to ignore are the ones you still believe. Which thoughts are compelling, believable, and therefore difficult to ignore? What negative thoughts come up again and again? What thoughts create the most feelings for you? Make a list of these problematic thoughts and investigate whether they

are true (they aren't) and where they might have come from (e.g., your father, mother, friends, the media). Did you realize that every single one of those thoughts is not true and doesn't serve any positive purpose? All those thoughts do is make you (and possibly others) miserable and maintain the false self, which you don't need.

LIVING FROM A PLACE OF TRUST

It's much easier to live in trust than not. Living in distrust of life is difficult and painful because it's a contracted and fearful place. Living in trust, on the other hand, is a place of openness, relaxation, receptivity, and flow. It's a place of not knowing what's coming next (we never do!) but not minding that we don't know. That's one of the biggest differences between how the ego relates to life and how Essence does. From ego, we want to know what we can't know and will never be able to know—what comes next. From Essence, we know that we don't need to know, so it's fine that we don't. We even enjoy not knowing.

The Being that we are doesn't want to know! It created life to be a mystery so that it could have an adventure. What fun to not know what's going to come out of the flow next! Can you find the place within you that feels that way? That is the antidote to the ego's fearful and contracted state of wanting to know but not being able to and then pretending to know as a way of coping with not knowing. How much easier it is to just accept the truth about life: We don't know very much, especially what's going to happen next.

Notice how you can relax when you let yourself not know. It's really safe to not know. The ego doesn't think it's safe, but not knowing is safe because something that is trustworthy and loving is at the wheel. The more we're in touch with our own loving nature—our true nature—the more we realize the nature of the universe—that it is safe and loving as well. Yes, there are creations in it that aren't loving, but what is behind it all is good.

Can you trust this? Can you let what is behind it all have its way with you and with all of its creations? Can you relax into this crazy, messy dance that is life? Craziness and messiness can be fun—not to the part of us that wants to know and wants to control life, but to another part of us. Can you feel life from the experience of Essence, as it lives through you?

Living from a place of trust is living from Essence, which naturally trusts what it's doing as it lives through us and trusts its capacity to respond to life wisely. If your only job were to respond to life lovingly, could you do just that? Do you think those responses would also be wise? Responding to life lovingly and wisely is our only task, but it requires a monumental leap from living from the ego to living from Essence.

Can you experience what is really living your life? What is here besides your thoughts? That is what can guide your actions and speech, and allowing that mysterious thing to move you is no more difficult than noticing that that is already happening and allowing it even more. You are already living from a place of trust much of the time: You jump out of bed and trust that the floor will catch you. You trust that your body will take in air when it needs it. You trust that air will be there for you tomorrow. Why not trust that your life will be the way it will be? Why let fear come in and frighten you about "your life"?

Your life is not yours, really. It is Life's, and life will have its way with you. You will dance with Life and work with it, but Life has a will of its own that shapes your life to some extent. Do what you can to shape life as you see fit, but also let it be as it is. When all is said and done, we are small players in this Grand Scheme. The more we can put our own lives and will in perspective, the more easily we can live in peace and in trust.

Living in trust is the experience of being in the flow—things happen naturally and easily, without a lot of thought. Trust is required to find the flow, to be in it, and to stay in it. But trust is not so much something you *do,* as something you stop doing—you stop distrusting, and then what's left is trust.

Not trusting is all that interferes with trusting and dropping into the flow. How hard is it to *not* do something? When it comes to *not* distrusting, it's just a matter of not believing a thought of fear or doubt. How hard is it to disregard a thought? We do this all the time, don't we? If you are able to see fearful and doubting thoughts for what they are (untrue thoughts), then you can disregard them, dismiss them, and give your attention to something else. What do you give your attention to instead? This beautiful moment and everything that's coming out of it—the flow. Living in trust is a matter of not giving our attention to fear and doubt, but to what is real and true here and now. How hard is that? How delightful is that?

Fear and doubts can be very compelling, so that is what inquiry is for. Through inquiry, we discover the misunderstandings and mistaken beliefs behind our doubts and fears, and that pulls the plug on their power. That saps them of their juice, their ability to mesmerize us and drive us. This is such important work. My wish for you is that you can joyfully embrace this work as you need to so that you can more fully be the free, loving, and peaceful Being that you already are.

* * *

I bow to God in gratitude, and I find the moon is busy doing the same
I bow to God in great happiness, and I learn from where the suns all borrow their light
I bow to the Friend in deep reverence and discover a marvelous secret carried in the air...
That this whole universe is just as blessed and loved as I
Just as wildly lost in this wonderful holy dance
At every step, gladly singing "Hallelujah!"
I hear the voice of every creature and plant singing the Beloved's name!
Every star and sun and galaxy, singing the Beloved's name!
All of God's creatures in the bosom of love, singing the Beloved's name!
Into your hands, I lay my spirit
Into your hands, I lay my life

From the song "Into Your Hands"
from *Open to Grace* by Peter Makena

ABOUT THE AUTHOR

Gina Lake is a spiritual teacher and the author of numerous books about awakening to one's true nature, including *Trusting Life, Embracing the Now, Radical Happiness, Living in the Now, Return to Essence, What About Now? Loving in the Moment, Anatomy of Desire,* and *Getting Free.* She is also a gifted intuitive with a master's degree in counseling psychology and over twenty years experience supporting people in their spiritual growth. Her website offers information about her books and online courses, free e-books, book excerpts, a monthly newsletter, a blog, and audio and video recordings:

www.radicalhappiness.com

Other Books by Gina Lake

(Available in paperback, Kindle, and other e-book formats.)

Embracing the Now: Finding Peace and Happiness in What Is. The Now—this moment—is the true source of happiness and peace and the key to living a fulfilled and meaningful life. *Embracing the Now* is a collection of essays that can serve as daily reminders of the deepest truths. Full of clear insight and wisdom, *Embracing the Now* explains how the mind keeps us from being in the moment, how to move into the Now and stay there, and what living from the Now is like. It also explains how to overcome stumbling blocks to being in the Now, such as fears, doubts, misunderstandings, judgments, distrust of life, desires, and other conditioned ideas that are behind human suffering.

Radical Happiness: A Guide to Awakening provides the keys to experiencing the happiness that is ever-present and not dependent on circumstances. This happiness doesn't come from getting what you want, but from wanting what is here now. It comes from realizing that who you think you are is not who you really are. This is a radical perspective! *Radical Happiness* describes the nature of the egoic state of consciousness and how it interferes with happiness, what awakening and enlightenment are, and how to live in the world after awakening.

Loving in the Moment: Moving from Ego to Essence in Relationships. Having a truly meaningful relationship requires choosing love over your conditioning, that is, your ideas, fantasies, desires, images, and beliefs. *Loving in the Moment* describes how to move beyond conditioning, judgment, anger, romantic illusions, and differences to the experience of love and Oneness with another. It explains how to drop into the core of your Being, where Oneness and love exist, and be with others from there.

Anatomy of Desire: How to Be Happy Even When You Don't Get What You Want will help you discriminate between your Heart's desires and the ego's and to relate to the ego's desires in a way that reduces suffering and increases joy. By pointing out the myths about desire that keep us tied to our ego's desires and the suffering they cause, *Anatomy of Desire* will help you be happy regardless of your desires and whether you are attaining them. So it is also about spiritual freedom, or liberation, which comes from following the Heart, our deepest desires, instead of the ego's desires. It is about becoming a lover of life rather than a desirer.

Return to Essence: How to Be in the Flow and Fulfill Your Life's Purpose describes how to get into the flow and stay there and how to live life from there. Being in the flow and not being in the flow are two very different states. One is dominated by the ego-driven mind, which is the cause of suffering, while the other is the domain of Essence, the Divine within each of us. You are meant to live in the flow. The flow is the experience of Essence—your true self—as it lives life through you and fulfills its purpose for this life.

Living in the Now: How to Live as the Spiritual Being That You Are. The 99 essays in *Living in the Now* will help you realize your true nature and live as that. They answer many question raised by the spiritual search and offer wisdom on subjects such as fear, anger, happiness, aging, boredom, desire, patience, faith, forgiveness, acceptance, love, commitment, hope, purpose, meaning, meditation, being present, emotions, trusting life, trusting your Heart, and many other deep subjects. These essays will help you become more conscious, present, happy, loving, grateful, at peace, and fulfilled. Each essay stands on its own and can be used for daily contemplation.

Getting Free: How to Move Beyond Conditioning and Be Happy. Freedom from your conditioning is possible, but the mind is a formidable opponent to freedom. To be free requires a new way of thinking or, rather, not thinking. To a large extent, healing our conditioning involves changing our relationship to our mind and discovering who we really are. *Getting Free* will help you do that. It will also help you reprogram your mind; clear negative thoughts and self-images; use meditation, prayer, forgiveness, and gratitude; work with spiritual forces to assist healing and clear negativity; and heal entrenched issues from the past.

What About Now? Reminders for Being in the Moment. The secret to happiness is moving out of the mind and learning to delight in each moment. In *What About Now*, you will find over 150 quotes from Gina Lake's books—*Radical Happiness, Embracing the Now, Loving in the Moment, Living in the Now,* and others—that will inspire and enable you to be more present. These empowering quotes will wake you up out of your ordinary consciousness and help you live with more love, contentment, gratitude, and awe.

For more info, please visit the "Books" page at
http://www.radicalhappiness.com

Made in the USA
San Bernardino, CA
20 February 2013